## YORK NOTES

# A Midsummer Night's Dream

## William Shakespeare

Notes by John Scicluna

 Longman       York Press

YORK PRESS
322 Old Brompton Road, London SW5 9JH

PEARSON EDUCATION LIMITED
Edinburgh Gate, Harlow,
Essex CM20 2JE, United Kingdom
Associated companies, branches and representatives throughout the world

First published 1998
Second impression 1999

ISBN 0–582–36835–9

Designed by Vicki Pacey
Illustrated by Gilly Marklew
Phototypeset by Gem Graphics, Trenance, Mawgan Porth, Cornwall
Colour reproduction and film output by Spectrum Colour
Produced by Addison Wesley Longman China Limited, Hong Kong

# ONTENTS

# PREFACE

York Notes are designed to give you a broader perspective on works of literature studied at GCSE and equivalent levels. We have carried out extensive research into the needs of the modern literature student prior to publishing this new edition. Our research showed that no existing series fully met students' requirements. Rather than present a single authoritative approach, we have provided alternative viewpoints, empowering students to reach their own interpretations of the text. York Notes provide a close examination of the work and include biographical and historical background, summaries, glossaries, analyses of characters, themes, structure and language, cultural connections and literary terms.

If you look at the Contents page you will see the structure for the series. However, there's no need to read from the beginning to the end as you would with a novel, play, poem or short story. Use the Notes in the way that suits you. Our aim is to help you with your understanding of the work, not to dictate how you should learn.

York Notes are written by English teachers and examiners, with an expert knowledge of the subject. They show you how to succeed in coursework and examination assignments, guiding you through the text and offering practical advice. Questions and comments will extend, test and reinforce your knowledge. Attractive colour design and illustrations improve clarity and understanding, making these Notes easy to use and handy for quick reference.

York Notes are ideal for:
- Essay writing
- Exam preparation
- Class discussion

The author of these Notes is John Scicluna, who, having studied English and Drama, began teaching in 1967. Since that time he has been actively involved in the teaching of English and English Literature to secondary age pupils.

The text used in these Notes is the New Penguin Shakespeare Edition, 1967, edited by Stanley Wells.

---

*Health Warning:* **This study guide will enhance your understanding, but should not replace the reading of the original text and/or study in class.**

# PART ONE

# INTRODUCTION

## HOW TO STUDY A PLAY

You have bought this book because you wanted to study a play on your own. This may supplement classwork.

- Drama is a special 'kind' of writing (the technical term is 'genre') because it needs a performance in the theatre to arrive at a full interpretation of its meaning. When reading a play you have to imagine how it should be performed; the words alone will not be sufficient. Think of gestures and movements.

- Drama is always about conflict of some sort (it may be below the surface). Identify the conflicts in the play and you will be close to identifying the large ideas or themes which bind all the parts together.

- Make careful notes on themes, characters, plot and any sub-plots of the play.

- Playwrights find non-realistic ways of allowing an audience to see into the minds and motives of their characters. The 'soliloquy', in which a character speaks directly to the audience, is one such device. Does the play you are studying have any such passages?

- Which characters do you like or dislike in the play? Why? Do your sympathies change as you see more of these characters?

- Think of the playwright writing the play. Why were these particular arrangements of events, these particular sets of characters and these particular speeches chosen?

Studying on your own requires self-discipline and a carefully thought-out work plan in order to be effective. Good luck.

*Family life*

On the 26 April 1564 William Shakespeare, the eldest son of John Shakespeare and his wife Mary, was christened at Holy Trinity Church in Stratford upon Avon. There is no exact record of the date of birth of William Shakespeare, but we can assume that it was only a few days before the christening and, by tradition, we normally celebrate his birthday on 23 April which is the Feast of St George. John Shakespeare was a glove-maker who was an alderman and later a bailiff of Stratford. John's wife, Mary, was the daughter of a local landowner called Arden. They had a total of three sons and four daughters, but only William's sister Joan is mentioned in his will, so it is possible that all the others died at quite a young age. William almost certainly attended the local grammar school, where he would have studied Latin and the Latin authors.

In November 1582 William married Anne Hathaway, a woman some eight years older than himself. Their first child, Susanna, was born in May 1583 and in 1585 they had a set of twins, Hamnet and Judith. Hamnet died when he was only eleven but the two daughters lived to marry and to have children of their own.

*His life in the theatre*

Little is known about what Shakespeare did to earn a living in Stratford, but some time in the late 1580s he must have left Stratford because by 1592 he was an established actor and playwright in London – and the target for jealous comments by an older, more experienced, writer called Robert Greene. Greene described Shakespeare as 'an upstart crow' who thought of himself as the 'only Shake-scene' in the country. Shakespeare worked mainly with a group of actors known as the Lord Chamberlain's Men, a group which later became the King's Men. The company included Richard Burbage who had the reputation of being the greatest actor of his time, and they performed at The Theatre, the first purpose built playhouse in England.

Shakespeare's early plays (1590–4) were *Henry IV Parts 1–3, Richard III, The Comedy of Errors, Titus Andronicus, The Taming of the Shrew, The Two Gentlemen of Verona, Love's Labours Lost, Romeo and Juliet* and *Richard II*. In 1596 he wrote *A Midsummer Night's Dream*, and by 1599, when the company moved to the new Globe Theatre, he had added a further eight plays. The next nine years (1599–1608) saw him produce some of his best known works including *Hamlet, Twelfth Night, Othello, Macbeth*, and *King Lear*. In 1608 the company became the King's Men. They took over the Blackfriars Theatre which had better facilities than the Globe, and they were also much in favour at court. The few plays that Shakespeare wrote in this later part of his life (1608–12) – *Pericles, Cymbeline, The Winter's Tale* and *The Tempest* – have happy endings.

As well as using verse forms in many of his plays, Shakespeare wrote poetry for its own sake. *Venus and Adonis* was published in 1593 and *The Rape of Lucrece* in 1594. *The Passionate Pilgrim*, which contains versions of some of Shakespeare's sonnets, was published in 1599 while *The Phoenix and the Turtle* was published in an anthology in 1601. As a poet he is perhaps best known for his Sonnets which were published in 1609.

*His later life*   Shakespeare did not lose touch with Stratford altogether. In 1596 he gained the right to a coat of arms and in 1597 he bought a very large house in Stratford called New Place. He bought further property in Stratford in 1602 and seems to have retired to spend most of his time in Stratford from about 1610. He continued to make visits to London and it was on one of these occasions, at the first performance of his play *Henry VII* in 1613, that the Globe theatre caught fire and burned to the ground.

Shakespeare died in Stratford upon Avon on St George's Day, 23 April 1616. He was buried in the

local church, where a monument on the north wall was
erected to commemorate the town's famous son.

## CONTEXT AND SETTING

*The rich and
powerful patrons
would sometimes
commission plays
for special
occasions.*

It is generally believed that Shakespeare wrote *A
Midsummer Night's Dream* as a special commission to be
performed at a wedding. Just whose wedding this might
have been is something of a mystery. It has been
suggested that it could have been the wedding of Sir
Thomas Heneage to the widowed Countess of
Southampton, but it was more likely to have been the
wedding of Thomas Berkeley to Elizabeth Carey.
Elizabeth was the daughter of Sir George Carey who
was the Lord Chamberlain, the patron of the company
of actors with whom Shakespeare worked. Whatever
the truth might be, Shakespeare would have kept in
mind the possibilities of performing the play for the
public afterwards. The humour of the play would have
been just as accessible to the uneducated 'groundlings'
who stood in the well of the Globe as it would have
been to the more sophisticated members of the original
wedding party.

Shakespeare used a variety of settings for his plays, so it
is not unusual to find that *A Midsummer Night's Dream*
is set in ancient Athens. Shakespeare would never have
been to Greece but he would have been familiar with
many of the mythological and historical characters of
that country. Many of his plays are based upon well-
known stories that he adapted to his own use, though it
is quite possible that the story of *A Midsummer Night's
Dream* is his own. In Elizabethan England most people
still lived, worked or had strong links with the
countryside. Folk stories and legends of fairies, ghostly
spirits and strange supernatural creatures were common,

*Shakespeare based
his plays on sources
from many
different
traditions.*

FOLKLORE                                        y

and so the fairy world of Oberon and Titania would not have seemed particularly strange to the audiences of that time. The title of the play and the mention in Act IV Scene 1 of 'The rite of May', are references to festivals of Tudor times. In many of these festivals the rules of ordinary behaviour were set aside, and the festivities might well include disorder and temporary changes in social status.

By using the wedding of Theseus and Hippolyta, two noble characters from classical Greek legend, as his starting point Shakespeare was able to give the play a feeling of importance beyond that of a simple **comedy** (see Literary Terms). Theseus and Hippolyta are larger than life figures whose meeting on the field of battle and subsequent marriage would have provided a powerful symbol for his audience. Their love takes on special meaning, firstly because of the dramatic and hostile nature of their first meeting and secondly because of the later perfection of their love – a love which brought about an end to a war. Shakespeare's audience would also have seen in their story an affirmation of the dominant role of the husband over the wife, an idea which they saw as a part of the natural law. Theseus himself makes his physical superiority over Hippolyta clear when he says:

*The theme of love provides opportunities for comedy and serious social comment.*

Hippolyta, I wooed thee with my sword,
And won thy love doing thee injuries; (I.1.16–17)

And a similar theme may be found in other Shakespeare plays, notably in *The Merchant of Venice* when Portia agrees to submit herself '... to be directed, / As from her lord, her governor, her king' (III.2.164–5), and in the *Comedy of Errors* when Luciana declares 'Men, more divine, the masters of all these... / ... Are masters of their females, and their lords:' (II.1.20–4)

*16TH CENTURY VIEWS on WOMEN*

Queen Elizabeth herself was, of course, unmarried, so she could still be her own 'master'! Shakespeare makes veiled references to the queen in this play; he mentions, for example, the goddess Diana who was untouched by Cupid's arrows but on the whole the play illustrates the Elizabethan belief that women had an inferior natural role to that of men. Such views may find little favour today, but the dominant nature of Theseus and his advice to Hermia – that she obey her father, use sound judgement in love and opt for marriage rather than the single life of a nun – would have struck very positive chords with the Elizabethan audience.

Similarly the rough and ready nature of the workmen, and their ham-fisted attempts at putting on a play, would have been very warmly greeted. It is interesting that Shakespeare seems to be poking fun at actors and playwrights, which he also does to some extent in *Hamlet* and in *Macbeth*. Perhaps he was saving the audience the bother of shouting out their own insulting comments!

*Purpose built theatres gave Elizabethans access to a new experience.*

An Elizabethan audience would have usually gone to the theatre in the afternoon. Specially built playhouses such as The Globe were a relatively new idea. These buildings had tiered galleries where the spectators could sit. This covered seating was built around an open area into which the stage, which had a balcony and a higher gallery, jutted out. Some of the audience would stand in the open area in front and round the stage. Since the theatre was quite small and the stage quite big, it meant that everyone could see and hear very clearly.

All the actors were male, so the younger actors would play the women's roles.

There was little scenery used, though the acting companies did spend large amounts on special effects, music and costumes. This meant that the audience had to use their imaginations rather more than we would expect to do today. It also meant that playwrights had to give their actors lines which would help to set the scene. In this play the main action takes place either at Theseus's court or in the woods. Do look at how many clues Shakespeare gives us about what the woods were like and about what time of day, or night, things happen. His use of the court helps to show the difference in status between the nobles – who are at home there – and the workmen – who clearly are not! The woods provide a strange and confusing environment for the four lovers and for the workmen, while being somewhere that the mystical fairies can seem perfectly at home. Theseus and Hippolyta are quite at home there when they are hunting in the daytime, but even then the hunt is heard rather than seen. The woods are, therefore, a place of hidden events, strange happenings and mysterious creatures. So Shakespeare creates an ideal setting for the strangeness and unreality of *A Midsummer Night's Dream*.

*The dialogue was important for setting the scene.*

# PART TWO

# SUMMARIES

## GENERAL SUMMARY

*Act I*

Theseus, the Duke of Athens, is preparing for his wedding to Hippolyta, Queen of the Amazons. He is approached by Egeus who wants his daughter, Hermia, to marry Demetrius. Hermia, however, is in love with Lysander. Theseus supports Egeus and tells Hermia that she must obey her father or suffer the consequences. Hermia and Lysander decide to elope. Hermia tells her best friend, Helena, of their plan. Helena, who is herself in love with Demetrius, decides to gain favour with him by telling him of the young couple's intended flight.

A group of Athenian workmen meet to cast a play which they hope to perform as part of the celebrations for Theseus's wedding. Despite one of the men, Bottom the weaver, wanting to play all the main parts they each receive their part and decide to rehearse their play in the woods, away from any possible observers.

*Act II*

In the woods, Oberon and Titania, the king and queen of the fairies, are involved in a bitter quarrel. Titania has refused to hand over to Oberon a young human boy that Oberon wants as his page. Assisted by his loyal servant, Puck, Oberon decides to avenge himself on Titania by casting a spell which will make Titania fall in love with the first creature that she sees when she wakes.

Demetrius has gone into the woods in search of Hermia. Helena has followed him. While Oberon waits for Puck to bring him the magic flower that he needs for his spell, he sees Demetrius treating Helena cruelly and rejecting her, while she passionately speaks of her love for him. Oberon decides to help her, and when

Puck returns with the magic flower Oberon directs him to find the Athenian couple and to use some of the flower's juice to put a spell on the young man so that on waking he will fall in love with the girl.

Titania's fairies sing her to sleep on a bank of flowers. Oberon creeps up to her and puts the spell on her. Expressing a wish that she should wake and fall in love with something horrible, he leaves her.

Lysander and Hermia are lost in the woods and very tired. They decide to sleep for a while. As they sleep, Puck stumbles across them and, mistaking them for the Athenian couple that Oberon had seen, he puts the magic spell on Lysander. Demetrius manages to shake off the chasing Helena and she sees the sleeping Lysander. Fearing that he might be injured or dead, Helena shakes him. Lysander wakes up and instantly falls in love with Helena. Helena believes his declarations of love are a cruel trick and she runs away from him. Lysander follows her. Hermia wakes to find herself alone in the woods and she sets off to find Lysander.

*Act III*      The workmen meet in the woods to rehearse their play. Their rehearsal is spotted by Puck who sees a chance for some good practical jokes. He bewitches the chief actor, Bottom, giving him an ass's head. All Bottom's friends run away from him, and Puck chases after them in different disguises. To keep up his spirits Bottom begins to sing. His song wakes Titania and she immediately falls in love with him. Titania and her fairies make a great fuss of Bottom.

Oberon is delighted when Puck tells him of Titania's love for the man with an ass's head. Puck also reports that he has put the love spell on the Athenian's eyes. Hermia has found Demetrius in the woods and she accuses him of killing Lysander. When Oberon recognises Demetrius, Puck realises he has made a mistake. Oberon is angry. Hermia runs off, Demetrius falls asleep and Oberon takes the opportunity to send Puck to bring Helena to that spot in the woods while Oberon puts the love spell on Demetrius. Lysander and Helena enter. Their voices wake the sleeping Demetrius and he too falls in love with Helena. Helena is now convinced that both the young men are involved in a cruel trick and are only pretending to be in love with her. When Hermia finds them, and Lysander still declares his love for Helena, she is sure that Hermia is in on the joke too. Hermia, on the other hand, is convinced that Helena has stolen Lysander from her. Demetrius and Lysander go off to fight over Helena, Helena runs away from Hermia and Hermia is left thoroughly bewildered by recent events. Oberon sends Puck to keep the young men apart, to tire them out and to bring all four young people to where they can fall asleep without knowing the others are close by. Puck does this. He then takes the spell off Lysander so he is no longer in love with Helena.

*Act IV*    Titania is still in love with Bottom. She fusses over him and they sleep wrapped in each other's arms. Oberon has asked Titania again for the changeling child, and this time she has handed the child over. Oberon now releases Titania from the spell and they are reconciled. Puck removes the ass's head, and returns Bottom's appearance to normal.

Theseus, Hippolyta and some courtiers are out hunting in the woods at dawn when they notice the four young lovers sleeping on the ground. When they are woken it is clear that Demetrius is in love with Helena and Hermia still wishes to marry Lysander. Theseus overrules Egeus, and he decides that the two couples will be married at the same time as Hippolyta and himself. None of the four young people are quite sure if the events of the night really happened or were merely dreams.

Bottom wakes up. He is surprised not to find the rehearsal still taking place, and he is so struck by the dream that he thinks he has had that he decides to have a ballad of his dream written so that he can recite it during the play.

Meanwhile, in Athens, the other workmen are bemoaning the loss of Bottom and the resultant ruin of their play. Bottom suddenly appears. He promises to tell them about his adventures but he announces that their play has been chosen and they must go to the palace to perform it.

*Act V*

Theseus chooses the workmen's play as the entertainment for the evening. The workmen perform their play, but they make many mistakes and act it rather badly. The courtiers are, however, entertained and frequently interrupt with comments. After the play, the actors are thanked for their efforts and they leave. The newly-weds retire to bed. Oberon and Titania bless the newly married couples while the fairies dance through the palace in a celebration of harmony.

| What happens | Who's involved | | |
| --- | --- | --- | --- |
| | Court & lovers | Fairies | Workmen |
| **1** Theseus plans to marry Hippolyta | ♥ | | |
| **2** Egeus complains about his daughter's disobedience | ♥ | | |
| **3** Hermia and Lysander decide to elope | ♥ | | |
| **4** Quince gathers his workmen to cast their play | | | 🖐 |
| **5** Argument between Oberon and Titania | | ✿ | |
| **6** Oberon decides to use magic | | ✿ | |
| **7** Demetrius chases Hermia and Lysander into the woods | ♥ | | |
| **8** Demetrius is followed by Helena | ♥ | | |
| **9** Oberon decides to help Helena | ♥ | ✿ | |
| **10** Oberon obtains and uses love-juice on Titania | | ✿ | |
| **11** Hermia and Lysander fall asleep and Puck mistakenly puts the love-juice on Lysander's eyes | ♥ | ✿ | |
| **12** Helena wakes Lysander who falls in love with her | ♥ | | |
| **13** Hermia wakes to find Lysander has gone, she looks for him | ♥ | | |
| **14** The workmen rehearse the play in the woods | | | 🖐 |
| **15** Puck gives Bottom an ass's head | | ✿ | 🖐 |
| **16** The other workmen run away from Bottom | | | 🖐 |
| **17** Bottom's singing wakes Titania and she falls in love with him | | ✿ | 🖐 |

| What happens | Who's involved | | |
| --- | --- | --- | --- |
| | Court & lovers | Fairies | Workmen |
| 18 Bottom enjoys the attention of Titania and her fairies | | ✿ | ✌ |
| 19 Oberon realises that Puck has made a mistake and given the love-juice to the wrong Athenian | ♥ | ✿ | |
| 20 Oberon scolds Puck and enchants Demetrius | ♥ | ✿ | |
| 21 Demetrius also falls in love with Helena | ♥ | | |
| 22 Hermia and Helena argue | ♥ | | |
| 23 Puck separates the four lovers and releases Lysander from the spell | ♥ | ✿ | |
| 24 Oberon gets the changeling child from Titania | | ✿ | |
| 25 Titania is released from the love-spell and she is horrified at Bottom's appearance | | ✿ | ✌ |
| 26 Oberon and Titania are reconciled | | ✿ | |
| 27 The Athenian lovers wake, and each couple is happily reunited and married | ♥ | | |
| 28 Bottom sleeps and wakes to find Titania gone | | ✿ | ✌ |
| 29 The workmen bemoan Bottom's absence | | | ✌ |
| 30 Bottom returns looking normal | | | ✌ |
| 31 The workmen's play is chosen and they perform it at the triple wedding celebrations | ♥ | | ✌ |
| 32 Oberon, Titania and the fairies celebrate and bless the human marriages | ♥ | ✿ | |

## ACT I

**SCENE 1**

Theseus, the ruler of Athens, and Hippolyta, Queen of the Amazons, discuss their forthcoming marriage. Theseus expresses his impatience, but Hippolyta calms him with the knowledge that the four days, till the new moon and their wedding day, will pass quickly. Theseus is determined that the wedding celebrations will be memorable and he sends Philostrate to encourage the Athenian people to organise festivities.

Egeus, a nobleman, enters with his daughter, Hermia. They are accompanied by two young men, Lysander and Demetrius. Egeus is angry that Hermia is stubbornly refusing to marry Demetrius, the man Egeus has chosen for her. Egeus accuses Lysander of having *Consider what* bewitched Hermia and so making her disobey her *Lysander has done* father. Egeus seeks Theseus's support, stating that *to bewitch* according to Athenian law Hermia must obey him or *Hermia. Do you* face death. Theseus tries to reason with Hermia, *think he has been* pointing out the danger her actions are placing her in. *wicked, or* He gives her four days to make up her mind to obey *romantic?* her father. Unwilling to condemn her to death, he warns her that refusal to marry Demetrius would

*Think about the
harshness of the
fate that faces
Hermia and what
that suggests to us
about the way
women were
regarded.*

mean that she would be forbidden from marrying
anyone else and she would have to spend the rest of her
life in a convent. Lysander points out that he is in every
way the equal, if not the better, of Demetrius. He
claims that he has more right to marry Hermia, saying
that she returns his love and that his love is true
whereas Demetrius is fickle since he had previously
declared that he loved Helena. Theseus leaves, taking
Egeus and Lysander with him for a private
conversation.

Lysander is left alone with Hermia. Bemoaning the
fact that 'The course of true love never did run smooth'
(line 134) they talk about the crosses that lovers have
to bear. Lysander reveals that he has a wealthy aunt
who lives outside the area covered by the laws of
Athens. He proposes that they should slip away that
night, meet in the woods and escape to his aunt's house
where they can be married. Hermia agrees to this plan.
Helena, Hermia's close friend, joins them. She is
unhappy and wishes that she were able to attract
Demetrius in the way that Hermia had done. Hermia
and Lysander tell Helena of their plan to elope, and
expressing the wish that Demetrius will come to love
Helena as much as she loves him, they leave. Helena
muses to herself about how blind love can be. She
decides that she will tell Demetrius about 'fair Hermia's
flight' (line 246).

COMMENT

Theseus and Hippolyta speak in a **lyrical** (see Literary
Terms) way about love and marriage, and introduce this
as a major theme of the play. Yet Theseus and
Hippolyta had faced each other on the battlefield when
Theseus had defeated the invading Amazons, and this
makes the suggestion, later clearly voiced by Lysander,
that 'The course of true love never did run smooth'
(line 134). As we meet each set of characters we usually
see that they are involved in conflicts of one sort or

another, but throughout the play we also see that conflicts can be resolved and that harmony can prevail.

As the slow passage of time is emphasised by words such as 'slow' and 'lingers', Theseus shows impatience for the arrival of their wedding day, which will be at the time of the next full moon. There are several references to the moon, throughout the play, which acts as a measurement of time for events and for characters. Night time is important as the time of mystery and dreams, and the moon **imagery** (see Literary Terms) that Shakespeare creates strengthens the dream-like quality of the events as well as reflecting the powerful influence of an outside force on the activities of man.

When Philostrate is sent to arrange festivities to celebrate the wedding, we are given the first mention of the ordinary Athenian people who will be represented by Quince and his group of workmen/actors.

Egeus's entrance strikes a note of discord. His manner is sharp and he refers to Hermia in terms that suggest his daughter is simply one of his possessions. This seems unacceptable to a modern audience, but might have seemed less so to an Elizabethan one. They would have viewed Hermia's youthful passion as less reliable than the objective view of an older and, therefore, wiser man! But much of the play does, of course, revolve around how unreliable and subjective love is. Both

*Make a list of the different conflicts that pairs or groups of characters are involved in when they first appear.*

Theseus and Egeus represent very strong figures of authority, and as a result they feel able to direct events and to make judgements without discussion. They behave in an autocratic way. Yet Theseus is also in love. He recognises Lysander's behaviour as being only what you might expect of a young man who is in love, and he does seem to have some sympathy with Hermia. He

warns her of the dangers of disobeying her father, but
he also offers her an alternative to the death penalty,
gives her time to think about her decision, and takes
Egeus and Demetrius away, presumably to discuss the
situation. His rather more even-handed approach helps
us to realise that the important thing is that conflict
exists, rather than which side we might take in an
argument.

When they are left alone, Hermia and Lysander
reflect on the misery and suffering that 'crossed' lovers
have to face, but Lysander's practical plan to run away
to his aunt's home appears to offer a quick and easy
solution. A plot, which seemed to be moving in
the direction of tragedy, is turned back so that
lightness and comedy can return. The lightness is
emphasised by Shakespeare's use of **rhyming couplets**
(see Literary Terms) from line 169 to the end of the
scene.

Helena's entrance shows another kind of suffering –
that of someone whose love is not returned. Helena's
confusion and lack of self-confidence about her
appearance is made clear in her first words. She makes a
**pun** (see Literary terms) on the word 'fair' since
Demetrius thinks that Hermia's dark complexion and
hair more 'fair' (beautiful) than Helena's natural fair
colouring.

The way the two girls respond to each other's words –
echoing them, reversing them – shows us their
friendship while at the same time highlighting the
differences in their situations. The closeness of the girls'
relationship is made clearer when Helena is told about
the plan to elope. By taking Helena into their
confidence, Hermia and Lysander also create the
possibility for all the chaos that the four lovers will face
later.

Helena's **soliloquy** (see Literary Terms) at the end of
the scene makes it clear that love is unreliable. It shows
us the blind and irrational nature of love that can make
someone see beauty where others would see none. This
prepares us for the effects of the love-juice on Lysander,
Demetrius and, of course, Titania. Helena's decision to

*Hermia's betrayal
by Helena is a
foretaste of her
betrayal by
Lysander.*

tell Demetrius what Hermia and Lysander are planning
shows us that she too is blind to the truth since
bringing Demetrius and Hermia together again is not
likely to improve her own chances of regaining the love
that Demetrius once had for her.

GLOSSARY

**nuptial hour**  wedding day
**apace**  quickly
**stepdame**  stepmother
**dowager**  widow
**revenue**  inheritance
**filched**  stolen
**wanting her father's voice**  lacking her father's approval
**the sealing day**  wedding day
**avouch it to his head**  say it to his face
**dotes in idolatry**  worships him as a god
**Steal forth**  creep away from
**translated**  transformed, changed

SCENE 2

A group of Athenian workmen – Quince the carpenter,
Snug the joiner, Bottom the weaver, Flute the bellows
mender, Snout the tinker and Starveling the tailor –
meet to cast and rehearse the play of Pyramus and
Thisbe. They hope to perform the play as part of the
Duke's wedding day celebrations. Quince seems to be
in charge, and he calls out the part which he wants each
man to act. Bottom, who is cast as Pyramus, interrupts
Quince several times. Bottom is keen. He shows off his
acting ability by reciting some lines in a 'tyrant's vein'
(line 36), and he is convinced he should also play the
part of Thisbe and that of the lion. Quince persuades

him he must play Pyramus. After each actor has his part, and they have agreed to meet again in the woods where they can rehearse secretly, they all exit.

COMMENT

Unlike the members of the court, the workmen's scene is written in **prose** (see Literary Terms). Shakespeare, and other Elizabethan playwrights, frequently use prose when writing scenes with ordinary, more humble, characters even when the rest of the play is written in verse.

*Consider what impression we gain of Bottom in this scene.*

The scene is a comic one. The humour comes mainly from the workmen's lack of understanding about how drama works. Bottom wants to play Pyramus, Thisbe and the lion, something which is clearly not possible. Quince is worried that Bottom would roar too ferociously and frighten the ladies, while Bottom claims that he could avoid that by roaring 'gently'. When Flute asks that he should not play a woman, we are reminded that in Shakespeare's time all the actors were male and so the younger actors played the women's parts.

Quince's tact is seen when he persuades Bottom that Pyramus is such a fine, handsome man that only Bottom can play him.

Another source of humour lies in the workmen's misuse of words, which they do not properly understand. Bottom says 'call them generally' (line 2) when he means 'call them individually'; he says 'I will aggravate my voice' (line 76) when he means 'moderate' it; he asks that they should rehearse 'obscenely' (line 100) when he means 'seemly'.

The title of their play, 'The most lamentable comedy and cruel death of Pyramus and Thisbe', is strangely contradictory. In part the title suggests that the tragic tale of Pyramus and Thisbe will be turned into something funny by the workmen's naïve acting of it, but it also suggests that comedy (see Literary Terms) – as we have already seen in the previous scene and as we will see in the distortion of love that follows – can have tragic or painful elements (see Themes).

GLOSSARY    scrip piece of paper with writing on it – a list
            treats on is about
            marry indeed
            extempore without a script, improvised
            con them study them, read them

**A** *Identify the speaker.*

1 'Full of vexation come I'

2 'If then true lovers have been ever crossed, / It stands as an edict in destiny'

3 'Call you me fair? That "fair" again unsay'

4 'Things base and vile, holding no quantity, / Love can transpose to form and dignity'

5 'Nay, faith, let me not play a woman – I have a beard coming'

*Identify the person 'to whom' this comment refers.*

6 'Stir up the Athenian youth to merriments'

7 'Be advised, fair maid: / To you your father should be as a god'

8 'But I beseech your grace that I may know / The worst that may befall me in this case'

9 'That's all one: you shall play it in a mask, and you may speak as small as you will'

10 'You may do it extempore; for it is nothing but roaring'

Check your answers on page 92.

**B** *Consider these issues.*

a Theseus's determination that his wedding day will be a memorable and happy occasion.

b The attitude of Egeus towards love and marriage.

c The ways in which Demetrius is not the right man for Hermia to marry.

d The seriousness of the situation created by Hermia's unwillingness to marry Demetrius.

e The ways that Shakespeare draws attention to the real love between Hermia and Lysander.

f The differences in character between Peter Quince and Nick Bottom.

g What we learn about the playwhich the workmen intend to perform.

# ACT II

SCENE 1

In the forest near Athens, night has fallen. Puck, also known as Robin Goodfellow, who is the servant to Oberon enters and meets a fairy who attends Titania, Queen of the Fairies. The fairy describes how she has been making flowers more attractive by putting sparkling drops of dew on them. Puck warns the fairy not to let Titania cross Oberon's path, as Oberon is angry. Titania has refused to hand over a human child that she is looking after and that Oberon wants as his pageboy. The fairy recognises Puck as a 'knavish sprite' (line 33) and she describes some of the practical jokes that Puck likes to play on people. Puck gives further examples of his tricks.

Oberon and Titania enter from different sides of the stage. Titania accuses Oberon of having had a love affair with Hippolyta, and Oberon responds by accusing Titania of being in love with Theseus. Titania describes the terrible effect their quarrel has had on nature and the seasons, then she details the destruction of the livestock and the crops on which mankind depends. When Oberon tells her that they can end their quarrel and put all these things right if she would only give him the boy, she explains that she can not do that. She values the child, who is the son of a devoted follower, too highly. Titania exits, and Oberon sends Puck to fetch a magic flower which, having been struck by one of Cupid's arrows, has juice that makes people fall in love. He intends to drop the juice into Titania's eyes while she is asleep so that when she wakes she will fall in love with the first creature that she sees.

Demetrius now enters, closely followed by Helena. He is looking for Lysander and Hermia. Oberon makes himself invisible and listens as Demetrius threatens

Helena if she will not leave him alone. Demetrius leaves and as Helena follows him Oberon promises to reverse the situation and make Demetrius love her more than she loves him.

Puck returns with the flower, and Oberon describes the place where he knows he will find Titania asleep. He tells Puck about the Athenian girl who is being badly treated by the young man she loves. Oberon gives Puck part of the flower, and tells him that while he is putting the love-juice on Titania's eyes Puck is find the Athenian couple. When the young man is asleep Puck is to put the love-juice in his eyes but to make sure that the first thing the young man will see when he wakes up will be the girl. Puck is told that he will recognise the man 'By the Athenian garments he hath on' (line 264), and neither he nor Oberon realise that there is another young Athenian man in the woods. Oberon tells Puck to meet him before daybreak, and they both leave to carry out their missions.

COMMENT

*Find other references to night in the play.*

References to night and moonlight by Puck, Oberon and Demetrius establish the night setting of the scene. The play would originally have been performed in the daytime in a theatre without the benefit of lighting effects (see Shakespeare's Background). The night-time setting is important since night-time is frequently associated with ideas of mystery, magic and insecurity. The mysterious effect of night-time, the woods and forces outside our control are the essential ingredients of the 'Dream'.

This scene introduces us to the fairies and the strange, mystical world in which they live. We learn that:
- Puck can change his shape and appearance, likes playing tricks and can move at great speed.
- Oberon can make himself invisible, has such keen eyesight that he has seen Cupid flying 'between the

cold moon and the earth' and that he understands –
and knows how to use – the magical property of
herbs and flowers.

- Oberon and Titania have a powerful influence on the
course of nature. Their quarrels have led to the
seasons losing their characteristic weather, causing
confusion and hardship in the world.

*Look closely at the
ways in which
Oberon's quarrel
with Titania has
affected nature.*

The quarrels have had an effect on nature and this has
affected the lives of human beings. This shows that the
world of the fairies may be different from that of man,
but it is not completely separated from it. This idea is
strengthened by the very human nature of the quarrels
over the changeling child and the jealousy that exists
over the alleged love affairs with humans.

Oberon's account of Cupid's unsuccessful attempt to
shoot a love-arrow into the heart of an 'imperial
votaress' (line 163) is possibly a reference to Queen
Elizabeth I who, having refused all offers of marriage,
was known as the Virgin Queen. The account is
dramatically important because it explains the creation
of the love-juice which will play such a vital part in the
events which follow.

It is clear that Oberon wants to humiliate Titania. He
wants her to fall in love with something ugly or
repulsive. Helena (I.1.232–3) has already alerted us to
the way that love can make something 'base and vile'
seem beautiful and attractive. The love-juice will have
that effect on Titania's view of Bottom. Helena's
entrance, as she pursues the unloving Demetrius, makes
us more aware of how blind and irrational love is.

Demetrius, in his search for Hermia and Lysander, is
angry to the point of insanity. His claim that he is
'wood within this wood' (line 192) is a **pun** (see
Literary Terms) on 'wood' meaning 'mad' and 'wood'
meaning 'trees'. It echoes the feeling that love makes

people behave irrationally, as does Helena's decision to follow Demetrius when common sense clearly suggests that she should not!

Oberon's **lyrical** (see Literary Terms) description of the bower where Titania sleeps paints a picture of a beautiful place where nature is 'luscious' (line 251) and 'sweet' (line 252). The many references to nature would have had a great appeal to the audience in a mainly rural Elizabethan society.

When Oberon sends Puck to put the love-juice in the eyes of a young man that he will recognise 'by the Athenian garments he hath on' (line 264) we have the beginning of the confusion. The audience knows that there is another young Athenian in the woods, but Puck and Oberon are unaware of this.

GLOSSARY      **thorough** through
              **anon** shortly, soon
              **train** attendants
              **hence** away
              **beached margent** sea-shore
              **governess** controller
              **hoary** white
              **progeny** children
              **as it** as if it
              **brakes** clumps of bushes
              **Fie** an expression of disgust
              **espies** sees

SCENE 2      Titania enters with her fairies. She gives them various tasks to perform and asks them to sing her to sleep. By the time they finish their lullaby, Titania is asleep and her fairies leave her alone. Oberon enters, puts the love-juice in her eyes and leaves.

Lysander and Hermia enter but do not see the sleeping Titania. They are lost and tired, and they decide to

*Puck's mistake starts off a confusing chain of events.*

sleep for a while. When Lysander seems about to sleep next to Hermia she begs him 'in human modesty' (line 63) to sleep a short distance away. As they sleep Puck enters. He sees Lysander in his Athenian garments and, mistaking him for Demetrius, puts the love-juice in his eyes and leaves.

Demetrius and Helena run on. Demetrius is still determined to lose Helena, and when he runs off she is too out of breath to follow. Helena does not see Hermia but she sees the sleeping Lysander. Fearing for his safety she wakes Lysander up and, under the spell of *The unreasoning nature of love is brought more strongly to our attention.* the love-juice, he instantly falls in love with Helena. Helena cannot believe his expressions of love and thinks that he is making fun of her. Upset by his unkindness she runs off. Lysander looks on the sleeping Hermia with contempt and leaving her asleep he chases after Helena. Hermia wakes, calling to Lysander for help. She has had a nightmare in which a snake has been eating her heart while Lysander looked on smiling. When she realises that Lysander is not there she is very frightened and sets off into the woods to look for him.

COMMENT    Titania's concern for beauty in nature is shown in her instructions to her fairies to kill the pests that spoil roses. Other fairies are sent to gather bats' wings to

*This scene further shows up the differences between Oberon and Titania.*

make coats for elves, and others to keep owls away. In Elizabethan times bats and owls were regarded as creatures of ill omen. The fairies are told to do all this in a 'third part of a minute' (line 2) and, like Puck's 'girdle round the earth / In forty minutes' (II.1.175–6), this suggests the speed at which fairies can travel.

The song that the fairies sing gives the audience a short musical interlude which adds to the magical quality of the setting. Although the song is about how the fairies will keep all evil, poisonous or harmful things away from Titania, the audience is aware of the **irony** (see Literary Terms) in that Oberon is waiting to do harm to her. Oberon's spell, and his grim hopes about what might happen when Titania awakes, make a stark contrast to the opening of the scene.

Lysander defends his attempts to lie down close to Hermia by assuring her of his good intentions and his faithfulness. Although he claims that 'lying so, Hermia, I do not lie' (line 58) when he is woken up he instantly declares his love for Helena. In doing that he is clearly being unfaithful to Hermia and his love for Helena is itself a kind of lie. Ironically the fact that Lysander and Hermia are keeping their distance while they sleep convinces Puck that he has indeed found the right couple.

The action of the scene moves quickly. Demetrius is so concerned with catching Hermia and shaking off Helena that he rushes off without even seeing the sleeping couple. Puck's mistake is rapidly brought to a head when Helena wakes Lysander so making him fall in love with her. Lysander claims that 'reason' has made him realise his love for Helena. Between lines 121 and 126 he mentions 'reason' four times, yet the audience know that 'reason' has nothing to do with his change of heart. By the end of the scene Lysander's apparent hatred of the innocent and sleeping Hermia is further evidence of how unreasoning his love is.

When Hermia wakes, her nightmare has clearly upset her deeply. The serpent eating at her heart is a powerful symbol of grief and despair at the outside force that has taken her love from her. Shakespeare shows us that while we may smile at the irrational behaviour of those who are under the influence of love, we must also recognise the pain felt by those who are hurt by it.

GLOSSARY     cankers  maggots

muskrose  briar, wild rose

offices  duties

beshrew  blame

fond  can mean both a) loving and b) foolish

marshal  one who leads or directs

Heresies  false beliefs

**A** *Identify the speaker.*

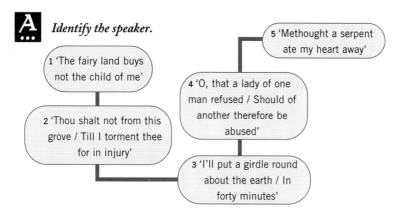

1 'The fairy land buys not the child of me'

2 'Thou shalt not from this grove / Till I torment thee for in injury'

5 'Methought a serpent ate my heart away'

4 'O, that a lady of one man refused / Should of another therefore be abused'

3 'I'll put a girdle round about the earth / In forty minutes'

*Identify the person 'to whom' this comment refers.*

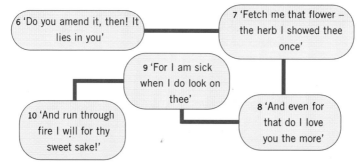

6 'Do you amend it, then! It lies in you'

7 'Fetch me that flower – the herb I showed thee once'

9 'For I am sick when I do look on thee'

10 'And run through fire I will for thy sweet sake!'

8 'And even for that do I love you the more'

Check your answers on page 92.

**B** *Consider these issues.*

a How Shakespeare prepares us for the confusion that the love juice will cause.

b How we should view Oberon's behaviour towards Titania.

c What view of Puck we might form from the description of the way he behaves.

d Your reaction to the feelings that Helena shows towards Demetrius, and his treatment of her.

e The different sorts of comedy that we can find in this Act.

# ACT III

## SCENE 1

*Examine how the simplicity of the workmen contrasts with the sophistication of the courtiers.*

The workmen enter the clearing in the woods where they intend to rehearse their play. Bottom is worried that the ladies of the court will be frightened when Pyramus draws his sword to kill himself. Starveling suggests that they leave the killing out, but Bottom has a solution – Quince must add a **prologue** (see Literary Terms) in which Bottom will explain that no harm is done with the sword, the character of Pyramus is not really killed and that Pyramus is only Bottom the weaver in disguise. Snout then asks if the ladies will not be frightened of the lion. Bottom rejects the idea of another prologue. He suggests that whoever plays the lion must introduce himself, show his face through a hole in the lion costume and carefully explain to the ladies that he is a man and not a real lion. The workmen then solve the problem of providing moonlight by suggesting that one of the cast can represent moonlight by carrying a bush of thorns and a lantern. The additional problem of having a wall through which Pyramus and Thisbe speak to each other is solved when Bottom suggests another actor can wear a costume covered in plaster.

*Look for times when Puck clearly enjoys his mischief.*

As they begin their rehearsal Puck enters. He is amused by what he sees. He decides to listen and, if the chance comes along, to join in the action. The actors rehearse, making a variety of mistakes in the pronunciation of words and in not giving each other the proper cues. When Bottom leaves the acting area and goes behind a bush to wait for his next entrance as Pyramus, Puck follows him. Puck puts a spell on Bottom so that when he re-enters he has an ass's head. The rest of the workmen are frightened by his appearance and they run off. Puck chases them and we gather he will further frighten and confuse them by changing his shape to

appear as a horse, a dog, a pig, a headless bear or a
flame. Snout and Quince each reappear briefly to tell
Bottom he is 'changed' or 'translated'. Bottom has no
idea of what has happened to his appearance and he
thinks his friends are playing some sort of practical joke
on him.

Left alone, Bottom tries to show he is not afraid by
singing aloud. His song wakes Titania who, under the
influence of the love-juice, falls in love with him. She
will not allow Bottom to even think of leaving the
woods, and she calls her fairies to look after him and to
bring him a selection of delicacies. Bottom introduces
himself to the fairies Peaseblossom, Cobweb, Moth and
Mustardseed, making a series of comments about each
of their names. Titania then makes her way to her
bower, ordering her fairies to lead Bottom there but
to 'Tie up my lover's tongue; bring him silently'
(line 196).

COMMENT

The simplicity, awkwardness and very ordinary
existence of the workmen are again shown by
Shakespeare's use of **prose** (see Literary Terms). The
prose contrasts starkly with the poetry and music of the
fairies in the opening of the previous scene.

*Find examples of
where the
workmen misuse
words.*

The workmen's mispronunciation and misuse of words,
and their fears that the audience will believe that the
characters and events in their play are real, reveals their
simplicity. It also hints at the exaggerated confidence
that ignorance can give to any of us. The workmen's
simplicity makes them easy targets for Puck's kind of
practical joke, and the ass's head that he puts on
Bottom reflects Puck's opinion of the workmen's
stupidity.

The workmen's play is written in verse. It is rhythmic
verse, which uses simple rhymes, but its use suggests
the social standing of the characters of Pyramus and

Thisbe. The poor quality of the verse suggests the poor job that these men are likely to make of producing a genuinely moving tragedy.

Bottom is unaware of his changed appearance. He is unnerved when his friends run away, and he tries to hide that fear by singing. When Titania wakes and declares her love for him, using words such as 'angel' (line 122), 'wise' and 'beautiful' (line 140), we realise how even someone as dignified and powerful as she is can be made a fool of love. This impression is strengthened when Bottom so readily accepts that anyone as beautiful as Titania can be so besotted by someone as rough and ready as him. Yet it is Bottom who so accurately observes that 'reason and love keep little company together nowadays' (lines 136–7). In that comment Bottom gives a clear reflection on what is happening in *A Midsummer Night's Dream*.

Bottom's acceptance of his place as the lover of the beautiful queen of the fairies, and the change that that brings about in his social standing, can be linked to the disorder frequently associated with popular festivals in Tudor times (see Context & Setting).

GLOSSARY     **bully** friend

**eight and six** a ballad form of poetry with alternate lines of eight and six syllables – Bottom's song 'The ousel cock...' (lines 118–26) is in this form

**defect** could mean a) effect or b) blemish, unfortunate result

**almanac** calendar

**loam** clay

**rough-cast** mixture of lime and gravel

**auditor** listener

**knavery** trickery

**enamoured of** in love with, attracted by

**enthralled to** captivated by, enslaved by

SCENE *2*

Oberon enters. He amuses himself by wondering whether Titania has yet woken, and what she might have fallen in love with. Puck enters and explains to Oberon how the workmen had met to rehearse the play and how he had placed an ass's head on the 'shallowest thickskin of that barren sort' (line 13) as he waited to make an entrance. He tells Oberon that when the other workmen had run away, Titania had woken and had immediately fallen in love with the ass. Oberon is pleased with Puck's work. Puck also tells Oberon that he has put the love-juice on the sleeping Athenian's eyes so he was sure to fall in love with the Athenian woman.

*Puck's mistake becomes clear and it leads to chaos.*

Demetrius enters with Hermia. Oberon recognises the young man and Puck realises he has made a mistake. Demetrius is still trying to persuade Hermia to love him but Hermia, convinced that Lysander would not have willingly left her alone in the woods, accuses Demetrius of having killed Lysander. She runs away from Demetrius who is now so tired that he decides to lie down and sleep for a while.

Oberon realises the mistake that Puck has made. He orders Puck to find Helena and to bring her to where Demetrius is sleeping. Puck leaves, and Oberon puts some of the love-juice on Demetrius's eyes. Puck, who seems pleased with the chaos his mistake is causing, returns saying that Helena is near at hand with Lysander following her and begging for her love.

Lysander and Helena enter. She is still resisting his advances. She tells him that the promises of love that he is making to her should be made to Hermia. Just as Lysander points out to Helena that while he loves her Demetrius does not, their argument wakes Demetrius who sees Helena and he instantly proclaims his love for her. Helena is now convinced that both the men are

teasing her and playing an unkind joke on her.
Lysander turns on Demetrius for being unkind to
Helena, saying he knows that Demetrius wants to
marry Hermia. In return Demetrius says that Lysander
can keep Hermia because his own love is 'home
returned' (line 172) to his first love, Helena.

*Both Helena and*
*Hermia feel*
*betrayed and*
*confused.*

Hermia enters. She has followed Lysander's voice
and is delighted to have found him. When Lysander
rejects her, Hermia appears confused but Helena
believes that Hermia is joining in the men's cruel joke.
She begs Hermia to remember their long friendship
and to stop the pretence. Hermia becomes more
'amazèd' (line 220) and says that it is Helena who is
scorning her, not the other way round. Still convinced
that she is the victim of a cruel joke hatched by all
three of the others, Helena decides to leave them.
Lysander begs her to stay and again declares his love
for her, as does Demetrius. The two men quarrel.
As Hermia tries to protect Lysander by holding him
back, Demetrius accuses him of being a coward.
Hermia now realises that Lysander is serious and that
she has lost his love. She turns on Helena accusing her
of deliberately stealing Lysander from her. The two
women quarrel, and Hermia claims that Helena has

used Hermia's lack of height as a way of making herself look better in Lysander's eyes. Hermia's growing anger frightens Helena, and she seeks the protection of the two men. The men's jealousy leads to a challenge and they leave to settle the quarrel once and for all. Hermia accuses Helena of causing all the trouble. Thoroughly frightened, Helena runs out followed by Hermia.

*We see how Oberon begins to put things right.*

Oberon sends Puck to create a fog to keep the young men apart. He tells Puck to prevent them from fighting, to lead them astray and to tire them out so that they fall asleep. Puck can then put another magic juice on Lysander's eyes, reversing the love-juice's spell and restoring his original love for Hermia. Oberon decides he will go to Titania and ask once more for the Indian boy so he can release Titania from the spell. Puck points out that dawn is approaching and all ghosts and wicked spirits must not be about in the daylight. Oberon reminds him that they are a different sort of spirit and so are not affected, yet he still wants to put things right before daybreak.

Oberon exits and as Lysander and Demetrius enter in turn, Puck disguises his voice so each man mistakes Puck for his rival. First Lysander and then Demetrius become exhausted and lie down to sleep. Helena enters. Unable to go any further in the dark, she too lies down. Moments later Hermia enters. Unaware of the others, she too lies down to sleep. Puck applies the new potion to Lysander's eye with the promise that 'all shall be well' (line 463) when they wake up.

## COMMENT

*Think about Puck's behaviour as a 'mad spirit'.*

Puck's account of Bottom's transformation, the workmen's reaction and Titania's falling in love with a 'monster' (line 6) clearly pleases Oberon. The vivid **imagery** (see Literary terms) that Puck uses, particularly that of wild geese and jackdaws scattering at the sound of a hunter's gun, makes the workmen's confusion and fear very real. Although a gun in the context of ancient Athens is an anachronism, the image of blind panic helps us to understand the workmen's belief that thorn bushes were living creatures grabbing at their clothes. The account of the confusion that Puck has caused among the workmen reminds us of what has happened and, with the appearance of Demetrius and Hermia, links that confusion with the confusion caused by Puck's mistake. When Oberon has placed the love-juice on the eyes of the sleeping Demetrius and Puck announces Helena's arrival we are ready for further confusion.

*Examine the expressions of love used by Lysander and Demetrius.*

Demetrius's first words to Helena, calling her 'goddess, nymph, perfect, divine' (line 137), are amusing as they contradict Lysander's claim that Demetrius does not love Helena. They also highlight again the irrational way that lovers behave. Demetrius continues with exaggerated descriptions of Helena's beauty. It is hardly surprising that Helena cannot understand the changes in the two men. Her belief that they are joined in a plot to make fun of her and that they both still love Hermia is perfectly logical.

*Consider Helena's right to accuse Hermia of betraying their friendship.*

It is clear, from Helena's recollections of their childhood, that she and Hermia were the closest of friends. Now it seems that Hermia has abandoned their 'ancient love' (line 215) and is involved in the plot. Although the argument between the four young lovers becomes increasingly heated and angry, we can still see it as comic because we are aware of how the misunderstandings began and we are also aware that Oberon is available with the power to put things right.

*Look for evidence to justify Helena's description of Hermia as a vixen.*

They will later wake and their confusion 'Shall seem a dream and fruitless vision' (line 371). The future return of harmony is made clear when Oberon expresses his belief that Titania will now hand over the Indian boy, be released from her love for Bottom and 'all things shall be peace' (line 377).

Puck ensures the safety of the four lovers by leading them in circles, keeping them apart and tiring them out. They lose sight of what is real and what is not – rather like the workmen whom Puck had led on 'in this distracted fear' (line 31).

Oberon makes it clear that he and the other fairies in this play are not like the damned spirits that cannot face the daylight. Shakespeare's audience might have needed reminding of this difference since they would have known many stories of wicked and dangerous spirits. Despite the difference that Oberon points out, the approach of Aurora, goddess of the dawn, is a welcome indication that the nightmarish madness of the night's events is rapidly coming to an end and that reality and sanity will return with the daylight.

GLOSSARY  in extremity desperately

dull drowsy, sleepy

shallowest thickskin having least brain but thick skinned like an animal

o'er shoes in blood wading in the blood of Lysander

O devilish-holy an oxymoron (see Literary terms) which suggests Lysander is using Christian symbols in an unholy way

congealed frozen

tame cowardly

juggler deceiver

counterfeit pretender

flout mock, make fun of

cheek by jowl side by side

death-counterfeiting sleep Shakespeare frequently uses this image of someone who is asleep looking like someone who is dead

wonted accustomed

spite injury

# TEST YOURSELF (Act III)

## A Identify the speaker.

1 'Not a whit, I have a device to make all well'

2 'What hempen home-spuns have we swaggering here'

3 'Bless thee, Bottom! Bless thee! Thou art translated!'

5 'O spite! O hell! I see you are all bent / To set against me for your merriment'

4 'When in that moment – so it came to pass – / Titania waked, and straightway loved an ass'

### Identify the person 'to whom' this comment refers.

6 'I pray thee, gentle mortal, sing again!'

7 'There is no following her in this fierce vein'

9 'Now I but chide; but I should use thee worse, / For thou, I fear, hast given me cause to curse'

10 'To what, my love, shall I compare thine eyne?'

8 'How now, mad spirit? / What night-rule now about this haunted grove?'

Check your answers on page 92.

## B Consider these issues.

**a** How the workmen solve the problems they foresee in performing the play.

**b** The appropriateness of Puck's trick on Bottom and the workmen.

**c** Bottom's reaction to Titania's love.

**d** The effect of Oberon's interference in the lives of the young Athenians.

**e** The differences between the way Shakespeare treats Helena and Hermia, as opposed to Demetrius and Lysander.

# ACT IV

**SCENE 1**

Titania enters accompanied by Bottom and several fairies. While she speaks lovingly to Bottom, Oberon watches secretly. Bottom, enjoying the attention, asks Cobweb to bring him a bee's honey bag while other fairies scratch his head to ease the itching. Titania offers him delicate music and food but Bottom prefers the coarse, simple music of the 'tongs and the bones' (line 29) and chooses to eat dry oats, hay and dried peas – as a donkey might. He feels tired and Titania, sending the other fairies away, cradles him lovingly in her arms. They sleep.

*Consider why Titania gives up the boy so easily this time.*

*Look carefully at the change in the relationship between Oberon and Titania.*

As Puck enters, Oberon tells him that he now pities Titania. She has given him the Indian boy and so Oberon determines to release her from the spell. He puts the antidote into her eyes. When she wakes she is filled with disgust at the sight of the creature with which she has been in love. Titania and Oberon are reconciled. Oberon orders Puck to remove the ass's head, restoring Bottom to his normal appearance. The fairies dance, and Oberon promises that all the pairs of lovers will be married the following night and their marriages blessed by the fairies.

As the fairies leave the stage, Theseus, Hippolyta, Egeus and the courtiers enter to the sound of hunting horns. Theseus describes the noise of the hounds as musical. Hippolyta agrees with him and recounts her memories of the sound of the Spartan hounds owned by Hercules. Theseus boasts that his hounds are descended from Spartan hounds and that their cries are matched like a peal of bells.

Theseus then notices the four lovers asleep. He remembers that this is the day on which Hermia is to give her decision about her future. He orders the hunting horns to be blown to wake the four young people up, and then questions them as to how Demetrius and Lysander, previously such bitter rivals, now seem to be friends. Lysander says that he cannot give a clear explanation. He admits he had gone to the woods with Hermia to escape from Athens so that they could marry. Egeus is angry and he repeats his earlier demand that his daughter should obey the law and marry Demetrius. When Demetrius explains that he loves Helena and no longer wishes to marry Hermia, Theseus decides he will overrule Egeus, and he invites the two couples to be married at the same ceremony as Hippolyta and himself. Theseus and the courtiers leave. The lovers seem confused about what has or has not really happened to them. They leave, saying they will each give their version of their 'dream'.

Bottom, now without the ass's head, has remained asleep and unnoticed by the others. When they have gone, he wakes up. He thinks he has had a short nap and is still in the middle of the rehearsal. He is surprised not to find his fellow actors around him. All his experiences with Titania and the fairies seem to him to have been a wonderful dream. He decides it makes such a marvellous story that he will get Peter Quince to write a ballad about 'Bottom's Dream' so that he can sing it as part of the play.

COMMENT Bottom is contentedly feeling at home as he enjoys the attentions of Titania and the fairies. His request that the fairies scratch his head, together with his choice of such food as dry oats and hay, shows us that his transformation has had a significant effect upon him.

References to music are important in this scene; they draw attention to harmony or discord in the relationships:

- Bottom expresses a preference for the rough and ready music of the 'tongs and the bones' (line 29). His choice creates contrast to Titania and the fairies whose music we know to be of a more gentle and refined nature. That contrast highlights the unsuitability of the match between them.

- Titania, on being restored by the antidote, calls for music 'such as charmeth sleep' (line 82). This mention of delicate, soothing music reflects the harmony that has been restored.

- Theseus refers to the sound of his hounds as 'musical confusion' (line 109) and Hippolyta, remembering her hunting expedition in Crete, declares that she never heard 'So musical a discord, such sweet thunder' (line 117). The strange pleasure of a sound that is a mixture of harmony and discord is a reflection of the bitter/sweet effect of love and of the mixture of harmony and discord which has affected the events in the play. Shakespeare's use of **antithesis** (see Literary Terms) matches the language to the mood, and from this scene onwards the discord gradually changes to harmony.

*Make a list of words which show harmony being restored.*

The surprise which Theseus experiences at finding the four young lovers together, with their quarrels apparently forgotten, is no greater than the surprise felt

by the four young people themselves. Lysander speaks
in a state 'Half sleep, half waking' (line 146) but this
refers to more than that half-awake state we can all
experience first thing in the morning! The nature of
events in *A Midsummer Night's Dream* leave the
characters unsure of what is real and what is not.

Theseus's decision to overrule Egeus and to allow
Hermia to marry Lysander, sets the seal on the new-
found harmony which the lovers are experiencing.
Demetrius's love for Helena is an after-effect of
Oberon's spell but we accept the rightness of it because:
* He had previously loved her
* His declaration of how much he now loves her (lines
  168–75) sounds more natural than the exaggerated
  expressions of love in Act III Scene 2
* We are pleased that after all she has gone through
  Helena will have the love of the man that she loves so
  much.

Bottom, now without the ass's head, has been forgotten
or unobserved. Perhaps that is the fate of the ordinary
man! He wakes believing he has only slept for a few
minutes. Bottom's humorous musings on what he
'dreamed' had happened to him, together with his
confusion over the functions of eyes and ears, make it
clear that a simpler, more popular humour will support
the play in its later stages.

It is worth noting that Bottom's words in lines 208–11
are a **parody** (see Literary Terms) of a passage from the
Bible: 'The eye hath not seen, and the ear hath not
heard, neither have entered into the heart of man, the
things which God hath prepared for them that love
Him' (1 Corinthians 2:9) which would have been well
known by the Elizabethan audience. They would have
seen such a parody as a gentle, but quite harmless, piece
of fun at the Bible's expense.

Bottom's determination that Quince should write a poetic version of 'Bottom's Dream' which could be added to the play of Pyramus and Thisbe, cleverly reminds us of how Bottom came to be involved in these strange events. It also reminds us that we still have the workmen's 'play within a play' to see, and forms a neat link with the next scene.

SCENE 2

*Notice how dependent the others seem to be on Bottom.*

The workmen meet in Athens. They are concerned that Bottom has not returned home and that they cannot perform their play without him. They are all convinced that Bottom would have been a great success, and Flute expresses the belief that Bottom would certainly have been well rewarded by the Duke. Just then Bottom returns. He promises to tell them of his adventures, but first they must get their things together and go with him to the palace where they are to perform their play.

COMMENT

*Compare the workmen's attitudes here with what they might have been thinking about Bottom earlier in the play.*

The workmen's faith in Bottom's ability is rather touching. Their conversation is only about how good an actor he was and the great success he must surely have enjoyed had the play been performed. It is rather like a group of people talking about someone who has died; everyone tries to say something nice about him!

Bottom's reappearance brings further harmony and happiness, and another bit of disorder and confusion is put right.

GLOSSARY

**marred** spoiled
**paragon** perfect example
**paramour** lover
**sixpence** a sum of money, six pennies, which was the equivalent of two and a half pence today, but a substantial amount in the sixteenth century

# TEST YOURSELF (Act IV)

**A** *Identify the speaker.*

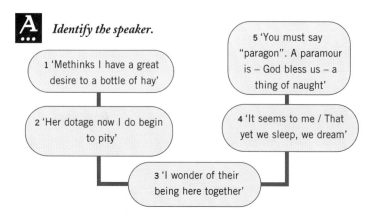

1 'Methinks I have a great desire to a bottle of hay'

2 'Her dotage now I do begin to pity'

3 'I wonder of their being here together'

4 'It seems to me / That yet we sleep, we dream'

5 'You must say "paragon". A paramour is – God bless us – a thing of naught'

*Identify the person 'to whom' this comment refers.*

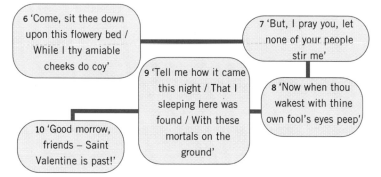

6 'Come, sit thee down upon this flowery bed / While I thy amiable cheeks do coy'

7 'But, I pray you, let none of your people stir me'

8 'Now when thou wakest with thine own fool's eyes peep'

9 'Tell me how it came this night / That I sleeping here was found / With these mortals on the ground'

10 'Good morrow, friends – Saint Valentine is past!'

Check your answers on page 92.

**B** *Consider these issues.*

**a** How aware Bottom is of the changes he has undergone.

**b** The evidence of Oberon's magical powers.

**c** The changes in Titania's feelings.

**d** What we learn about the relationship between Oberon and Titania.

**e** The qualities Theseus displays.

**f** The sort of conversation the four lovers are likely to have on their way back to Athens.

**g** The change of mood Bottom's reappearance brings about.

# ACT V

SCENE 1

*Theseus and Hippolyta react differently to the lovers' story.*

The weddings of Theseus and Hippolyta, Lysander and Hermia, and Demetrius and Helena have taken place. Theseus and Hippolyta, accompanied by some of the court, enter. Hippolyta talks of the 'strange' (line 1) events that the lovers have spoken of. Theseus puts it all down to fantasies created by over-keen imaginations spurred on by love. Hippolyta thinks it odd that all four tell the same story. The four lovers enter, and all greet each other with hopes of joy for the future.

Philostrate, Theseus's Master of the Revels, is called to explain what entertainment is available. He has a list that contains: a song about the battle with the Centaurs; a play describing the tearing of a Thracian singer to pieces by the drunken worshippers of Bacchus, the god of wine; a satirical piece about the nine Muses mourning for the death of Learning; and the 'tedious brief' (line 56) play which the workmen have prepared. Philostrate, who has seen a rehearsal of the play, warns Theseus against seeing the workmen's ridiculous attempts at acting. Hippolyta also discourages him as she hates to see people make fools of themselves by struggling to do what is beyond their abilities. Theseus, however, rejects all the other items for various good reasons. He says that good intentions deserve to be recognised even if the performances leave something to be desired. The workmen's play is chosen.

Quince enters and speaks the **Prologue** (see Literary Terms), but is so nervous that he misplaces the punctuation and so distorts the meaning of what he is trying to say. Bottom, as Pyramus, Flute as Thisbe, Snout as Wall, Starveling as Moonshine and Snug as Lion, all enter. They perform a mime while Quince gives a simple account of the plot. All the actors, except

*Theseus and the courtiers interact with the players.*

Snout, leave. The play begins, and throughout it the court audience interrupts with witty comments on the acting and the action. Snout explains that he is the wall that separates the two lovers, Pyramus and Thisbe, and that his fingers represent the hole through which the lovers whisper to each other.

Pyramus enters, making a fuss because he believes Thisbe has not kept her promise to meet him. Thisbe enters and, through the hole in the wall, she and Pyramus arrange to meet at Ninus's tomb. When they leave, Snout explains that the wall has done his part and so he too leaves. The lion and Moonshine now enter. Snug makes a brief speech explaining he is not a real lion but only Snug the joiner. Starveling is put out by the comments being made by the audience. After two false starts he manages to blurt out a brief explanation of how he, the lantern, the thorn bush and the dog represent the Moon. Thisbe enters for her meeting with Pyramus at Ninus's tomb. She is frightened by the lion, and as she runs off she drops her mantle which the lion attacks and tears with his bloodstained teeth. Pyramus enters. He thanks the moon for lighting his way, but then finds the torn and bloodstained mantle. Assuming that Thisbe has been killed by the lion, Pyramus draws his sword, stabs himself, orders the moon to leave, and dies. Thisbe returns, finds Pyramus dead, and after what is supposed to be a tragically moving and poetic lament over his body, stabs herself. Bottom leaps up from the dead and asks whether Theseus would like the entertainment to end with an epilogue or a simple country dance known as a Bergomask. Theseus thanks them for their play, and asks for the dance. When the dance has been performed and the actors have left the stage, the clock strikes midnight and Theseus declares it is time for bed.

When all the courtiers have gone, Puck enters. He says that now, while the mortals are asleep, the creatures of the night can come out and 'frolic' (line 377). He is followed by Oberon, Titania and the fairies. They sing and dance. Oberon blesses the newly-weds to ensure that their children will be born healthy with no blemishes or scars. Everyone leaves, except for Puck who speaks directly to the audience. He hopes that the performance has pleased the audience but if it has not he reminds them that the actors are only 'shadows' (line 412) and what the audience has watched no more real than a dream. Asking for applause, he exits.

*Oberon cements the sense of harmony.*

## COMMENT

*List the strange things Theseus claims might be seen by madmen, poets and lovers.*

Theseus's first speech shows he has little faith in the story the lovers tell. He dismisses stories of fairies as old fashioned and absurd, labelling them 'antique fables' and 'fairy toys' (line 3). His argument is that lovers, madmen and poets are all victims of overactive imaginations and they believe they see things that a calm, sensible person would not. Theseus is making a dramatic statement about the power of the imagination which, as he concludes, can make us mistake a bush for a bear. That same power of the imagination is vital for the audience of the play, and was even more vital for an Elizabethan audience when plays had so little scenery to aid imagination. Hippolyta's reaction to the lovers' story is less dismissive. Though she finds their story strange, the similarities in what each of the lovers had experienced makes her feel that the stories should be believed. Shakespeare gives us both sides of the argument and leaves us to make our own decision.

Shakespeare presents us with an interesting **irony** (see Literary Terms) for while Theseus condemns 'antique fables' he is himself a mythical hero whose exploits are referred to in the play. Theseus was supposedly descended from Poseidon, the sea god, and he brags about being related to the demi-god Hercules – so he was himself a part of the 'antique fables' that he condemned.

*Examine the way in which the workmen's play is written.*

The workmen's play is chosen despite Philostrate's damning, but witty, description of it. The workmen are naïve, and they understand the ideas of theatre far less well than do the audience in the theatre or the courtly audience on the stage. Shakespeare uses their lack of sophistication as an important method of bringing out the **comedy** (see Literary Terms) in this Act. The workmen/actors are at pains to point out that what is being performed is an illusion and not any sort of reality. They have little idea of what is really effective in staging a play. The response of the courtiers tells us that the acting was bad. The play of 'Pyramus and Thisbe' is crudely written in poor verse using some terrible rhymes, unnecessary repetitions, exaggerated use of **alliteration** (see Literary Terms) and such ridiculous **similes** (see Literary Terms) as 'His eyes were green as leeks' (line 325). Quince's nervous distortion of his **Prologue** (see Literary Terms), Starveling's loss of temper, Bottom's impromptu reply to Theseus's comment about the wall and his explanation of what is to happen shortly, all lead up to Pyramus's magical rising from the dead to ask how Theseus would like the entertainment to conclude!

The theatre audience is able to enjoy not only the workmen's comic attempt at illusion in their 'play within a play', but the genuine illusion created by *A Midsummer Night's Dream*.

When the clock strikes midnight, the court retires. It is the hour for magic. Oberon and Titania, now in perfect harmony, dance and give their blessing as an assurance that, whatever has happened in the past, the future will be happy and secure. Puck's final speech invites the audience to regard him and the other actors as 'shadows' (line 413) in a 'dream' (line 418). This reminds us that, just as the characters have been bewitched and have been subject to an illusion, so we too have been involved in an illusion. His request that the audience should give him their hands is not simply an invitation to shake hands but a request that the audience should give their applause and so end the performance.

GLOSSARY      **bodies forth**  gives shape to
              **sport**  entertainment
              **take what they mistake**  understand or accept what they do badly
              **saucy**  impertinent
              **audacious**  bold
              **stand upon points**  take notice of punctuation
              **sunder**  keep apart
              **mantle**  shawl or cloak
              **broached**  pierced
              **befall**  happen
              **Fates**  three sisters in Greek mythology who controlled each
                person's birth, life and death
              **Furies**  in Greek mythology, three ferocious goddesses who
                punished wrongdoers
              **solemnity**  celebration (of the wedding)
              **blots of Nature's hand**  deformities
              **reprehend**  find fault
              **scape**  escape

# TEST YOURSELF (Act V)

**A** *Identify the speaker.*

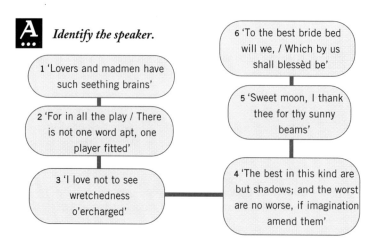

1 'Lovers and madmen have such seething brains'

2 'For in all the play / There is not one word apt, one player fitted'

3 'I love not to see wretchedness o'ercharged'

6 'To the best bride bed will we, / Which by us shall blessèd be'

5 'Sweet moon, I thank thee for thy sunny beams'

4 'The best in this kind are but shadows; and the worst are no worse, if imagination amend them'

*Identify the persons 'to whom' this comment refers.*

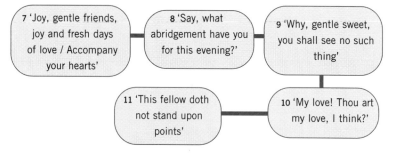

7 'Joy, gentle friends, joy and fresh days of love / Accompany your hearts'

8 'Say, what abridgement have you for this evening?'

9 'Why, gentle sweet, you shall see no such thing'

11 'This fellow doth not stand upon points'

10 'My love! Thou art my love, I think?'

Check your answers on page 92.

**B** *Consider these issues.*

**a** The use made of the variety of verse in Act V.

**b** The difference between what Quince says in his first speech and what he intended to say.

**c** The level of success achieved by the workmen in putting on their play.

**d** How the comments made by Theseus and the others during the workmen's performance add to the humour.

**e** The impression of night-time created by Puck's speech (lines 361–80).

# PART THREE

# COMMENTARY

## THEMES

### LOVE

Most of Shakespeare's comedies are, in one way or another, concerned with love and with the problems frequently associated with it. In this play there is a clear difference made between the natural state of mature and genuine love and the illusion generated by a love that has no substance. Love is certainly an emotion, but the play suggests that the emotion needs to be balanced by reason. The mature love of Theseus and Hippolyta, a love forged in early conflict and adversity, is passionate – but it is also a bond between sensible and mature adults. Such a love, enshrined in marriage, should produce harmony, but when fickle lovers quarrel – as Oberon and Titania do – that quarrel will create a wider discord.

Nothing can stand in the way of true love, even though its path may not be smooth. Hermia and Lysander are prepared to leave friends, home and family in order to be married, and Pyramus and Thisbe die for love of each other. Yet love can be a somewhat foolish thing. Doting on someone, as opposed to loving someone deeply, leads to irrational behaviour. Diana may be the goddess of the hunt, but she is also a powerful symbol of chastity, moderation and self-control. Theseus and Hippolyta, through the hunting scene in Act IV, are linked to her attitudes. However, Cupid, the god of love, is described by Helena as a blindfolded child irresponsibly playing tricks. The exaggerated language of those under the love-spell that Oberon creates from the flower hit by Cupid's arrow certainly highlights how irresponsible and irrational their behaviour is. Titania tells Bottom that she has been moved 'On the first view to say, to swear, I love thee' (III.1.134), and Lysander has declared instant love to Helena saying 'run through fire I will for thy sweet sake!' (II.2.109). It is the simple, but unbewitched, Bottom who reminds us that 'reason and love keep little company together nowadays' (III.1.136–7). Lysander's claim that his new-found love for Helena is a result of his reason is as plainly ridiculous as is Demetrius's assertion that his heart has willingly returned 'home' to her. The love-juice influences the behaviour of the characters, and the idea works because we can all appreciate the fickle nature of infatuation.

*Look at which pairs of lovers remain constant, and which change their affections.*

Love can create jealousy. The jealousy between Oberon and Titania has caused disruption and discord in the world. On a lesser level, the jealousy between the four lovers has caused such discord that Hermia and Helena abandon their lifelong friendship, betray each other and quarrel in a spiteful and abusive way, while Lysander and Demetrius develop more than a passing fancy to kill each other! When jealousy is put aside and the lovers marry, we see a return to the romantic notions of a true and lasting love.

## DISCORD AND HARMONY

Closely linked to the theme of love is that of the creation of discord and harmony. The Elizabethans believed that order was a vital component in both the natural world and human life. Proper respect for lawful authority and for the order that such authority created was very important to them. There was a balance in the world, which order maintained and when proper order was disregarded that balance was upset with terrible consequences. Shakespeare used that idea powerfully in his play *Macbeth* where the human chaos created by the destruction of lawful order when King Duncan was murdered is reflected by chaos, unnatural events and storms in the natural world.

In this play there are frequent quarrels, disagreements and betrayals. Egeus quarrels with Hermia; Helena betrays Hermia; Puck's mistake leads to misunderstandings and violent arguments between the four lovers. The quarrel between Oberon and Titania has not only resulted in the destruction of crops and the misery associated with unseasonal weather, but will also set off the harmful chain of events in which the humans in this play find themselves entangled. But Oberon's decision to bewitch Titania is for a specific and limited purpose; should he succeed in gaining the boy from her then the reason for their initial quarrel will disappear. So the play is not only about discord; it is also about a progression from discord to harmony, from a state of chaos to one of order. We usually associate the words

*Consider the* discord and harmony with music, and there are several
*occasions when* occasions in the play when music, singing and dancing
*music is mentioned* are all used to introduce a note of happiness. Music is
*or used, and the* used, or mentioned, frequently in scenes involving the
*effect that the* fairies and you might have noticed that in the latter part
*music creates.* of the play, as the plot moves from chaos/disorder towards order/harmony, the musical interludes are more frequent.

## AGE AND YOUTH

The differences in attitude between young and old are first shown in the behaviour of Egeus and his daughter, Hermia. Egeus feels he has the right to insist on directing the course of Hermia's life irrespective of her own wishes and feelings. He has the law – the idea of good order – on his side, and he dismisses her reluctance as evidence of stubbornness brought on by

Lysander's cunning manipulation of her youth and inexperience. The tricks that Lysander is accused of using were simply the writing of love poems, singing of love songs and giving of small presents as tokens of his love. All of these things were quite normal ways for an Elizabethan gentleman to show his love for the lady of his choice. They may not be exactly what a young man might do today, but we can all recognise something similar in modern relationships. The reactions of Hermia and Lysander to what Egeus and Theseus say to them indicate their love is genuine, but Egeus sees it as insincere and accuses Lysander of 'feigning love' (I.1.31).

Theseus is a symbol of both age and order. Though he is more mature than Hermia and Lysander he is newly in love and so has considerable sympathy for them. His status as the upholder of the law, however, puts him in a difficult position. While he is prepared to spare Hermia from death he is not, at the beginning of the play, prepared to set aside her father's rights under the law. Later on, when he sees that the lovers have resolved their differences so that Demetrius no longer wishes to make any claim on Hermia, Theseus is able to change sides and allow his sympathy with the young to overrule his sense of duty to the old.

*Think about how the Elizabethan 'Generation Gap' is similar to, or different from, modern attitudes of young and old.*

While Theseus might be able to see both sides of the argument, we are in little doubt that the young will not see things through the eyes of the old. They will not 'choose love by another's eyes' (I.1.140) and Egeus is unlikely to comply with Hermia's desire that 'I would my father looked but with my eyes' (I.1.56). The generations would not see eye to eye and Hermia's determination to become a nun, or even to be put to death, rather than marry a man she does not love strikes a sympathetic chord. We feel that Egeus and the older generation surround themselves with attitudes that

restrict the freedom which the younger generation
desperately seeks.

## GREEK MYTHOLOGY

*Ancient beliefs in*
*a variety of gods*
*are a rich source of*
*ideas for*
*Shakespeare's*
*plays.*

We must be careful not to think that this play is
actually about Greek mythology. The references to
characters from mythology help to set the scene and
provide useful reference points. The Elizabethan
audience would have been more familiar with
mythological characters than most people might be
today. Theseus and Hippolyta feature in Greek legend.
Theseus was famed for his bravery. He captured the
fire-breathing bull of Marathon, slew the Minotaur and
helped to defeat the Centaurs – creatures that were half
man and half horse. It was in his defence of Athens
against the invading Amazons, a tribe of fierce female
warriors, that he met and fell in love with the Amazon
Queen, Hippolyta. Theseus and Hippolyta make a
useful example of mature love against which to set the
chaotic events generated by Oberon's use of the love-
juice.

In the play there are references to many Greek (and
Roman) gods:
- Diana was the Roman goddess of the moon, hunting
  and chastity. Shakespeare also refers to her by her
  other name, Phoebe
- Venus was the goddess of Love and Cupid the child-
  like god whose arrows pierced the heart to cause the
  'victims' to fall in love
- Apollo was the god of the Sun, also known as
  Phoebus (whom Bottom mistakenly calls Phibbus)
- Hecate, a mysterious goddess with influence over
  heaven, earth and hell, was usually portrayed as
  having three heads. She was regarded as an evil deity
  and was thought to command the evil spirits

- Bacchus was the god of wine
- Neptune, or Poseidon, the god of the sea
- Aurora was the goddess of the dawn
- The Fates were three sisters who controlled each man's birth, life and death
- The Furies were the three goddesses who punished all wrongdoers

These references are all used in the play to indicate forces which are outside human control yet which influence aspects of human life.

Mention is made of the ancient cities of Athens, Sparta and Thebes and the region of Thessaly. Mythological heroes and lovers are also mentioned. Among these are Corin and Phillida. Titania accuses Oberon of disguising himself as Corin in order to flirt with Phillida. Oberon responds by dragging up Titania's affection for Theseus while reminding Titania of Perigeria, Aegles, Ariadne and Antiopa – all of whom were former lovers of Theseus. The play of 'Pyramus and Thisbe' is based on those two Babylonian lovers. Pyramus and Thisbe meet at the tomb of Ninus, who was the founder of Babylon. As with the references to gods and goddesses, some of these references help to create images which boost the impact of the events taking place. They also set the events within a clear context, but more importantly they add an essentially mysterious, unreal, dream-like quality to the events.

## NIGHT AND THE MOON

*Look for the different occasions when darkness or the moon are mentioned.*

For many scenes the darkness brought by night is an essential ingredient. Night is when humans usually sleep and when magical beings are about. We do not see very well in the dark, and that physical inability to see clearly is a parallel to the inability to understand when we are confused. While the fairies feel at home in the dark, the human characters do not. They become lost and frightened, and, as Oberon and Puck manipulate their emotions, they lose their true identities, seeming to change their appearance, attitudes and affections from scene to scene. Shakespeare uses the contrast between daylight and darkness, and the importance of being able to see clearly and to believe what we see, to reflect the states of knowledge and ignorance through which the characters pass. For much of the play they do not know or understand what is going on – they are 'in the dark'; with the daylight comes the revelation of a kind of truth, an ability to see and an inclination to put their trust in what they see. No longer are bushes seen as bears.

The moon and its light figure prominently in the play. Moonlight is very different from daylight, and the moonlight creates a magical and mysterious world in which natural forms are disguised. The full moon was said to affect people's behaviour, to make them mad. Indeed the word 'lunatic' stems from the Latin for 'moon'. The behaviour of the characters during the moonlit scenes is unnatural and irrational.

At the beginning of the play the moon is described as 'like to a silver bow / New-bent in heaven' (I.1.9–10). This powerful image of a weapon ready to fire its destructive missile at the world is an apt way of introducing the madness that will follow.

### THE NATURAL WORLD

The world of nature is, in this play, shown as being a place of great beauty and an area of potential danger. The place where Titania sleeps is an enchanting bower where fragrant flowers grow. Yet it is in the woods, a wild place where Bottom and the lovers can feel lost and afraid. The woods are a place of mystery and magic, closely associated with the fairies. They are also a place where snakes, spiders, beetles, bats and other creatures, believed to be or actually dangerous, can threaten the peace of even one so powerful as Titania. Oberon speaks of such fearsome creatures as lions, bears and wolves – creatures that can be hunted in daylight by Theseus and his hounds but which would present real danger at night. Nature is full of life and anyone who is familiar with the countryside will know that there you are surrounded by vast numbers of creatures of assorted shapes and sizes even when you cannot see them. Nature helps us to survive, to grow our crops and to feed our animals, but it can also be cruel, unpredictable and destructive.

*Elizabethans were very conscious of the parallels between human life and the natural world.*

The colours Shakespeare mentions, from the cold, pale light of the moon which distorts and confuses to the fiery red glow of the dawn which warms and comforts, affect our feelings and perceptions. The colours of ravens and doves, spotted snakes with enamelled skins, milk-white and purple flowers, and even the cherry nose and yellow cowslip cheeks of Pyramus, all create images and enhance contrasts. The way that the natural world can be harmonious and balanced is an example to the human world; but just as the human world can suffer discord and unrest, so the natural world can be unbalanced and dangerous.

## IMAGINATION AND ILLUSION

*Consider the range of illusions that are presented to us during the play.*

Every play depends upon creating an illusion with the help of the imagination of the audience. A well-worked illusion can seem real. In this play there is confusion among the characters as to what is real, and what is not. They spend their time in a dream-like state where reason is clouded and they are no longer sure of themselves or of the reality they think they see. It is interesting to notice how often characters sleep in this play. When we sleep we frequently experience dreams that seem so real to us that we can wake confused and frightened. Shakespeare uses sleep as a convenient way to enable Oberon to cast his spells and either to create or to sort out problems. Yet when the characters wake their ideas of what is real are changed, and they have the same confusion that we might experience through having a dream. That confusion is heightened because the reality that they are experiencing has also changed – they fall in and out of love or they grow monstrous heads!

Oberon creates the illusion of love, and the belief that Lysander and Demetrius have in that illusory love causes chaos. Puck disguises himself and creates the illusions that the workmen are being chased by wild creatures or that Demetrius and Lysander are chasing each other when they are really following Puck's voice. We, the audience, can smile at these illusions, as we can at the workmen's attempts to create an illusion through their play of 'Pyramus and Thisbe'. Yet we too are involved in the illusion which is theatre, for while we watch the characters being tricked we easily lose sight of the fact that those characters only live because we let them live in our imaginations.

## STRUCTURE

*Get a clear idea of how the characters are grouped and of where different groups interact.*

In his plays Shakespeare normally has a central plot beneath which we can find one, or more, **sub-plots** (see Literary Terms). It is usually quite easy to recognise the main plot and to see how the sub-plots fit in with it. In *A Midsummer Night's Dream*, however, we have three quite distinct groups of characters whose activities form four plots of more or less equal importance. The three groups of characters are the courtiers, the workmen and the fairies. The courtiers are involved firstly in the plot-line surrounding the wedding Theseus and Hippolyta, and secondly in the tangled love affairs between Hermia, Lysander, Demetrius and Helena. The workmen's planning, rehearsal and performance of the play 'Pyramus and Thisbe' forms the third plot, while the theme of the quarrel between Oberon and Titania gives rise to the fairies' plot. Each of these four strands of the play inevitably crosses and links with each of the others as the groups come into contact with each other, knowingly or unknowingly. Shakespeare makes full use of the possibilities opened up by the very different kinds of characters within each group and the different dramatic opportunities offered by the situations in which they are involved. The groups contrast vividly: the sophisticated, yet earth-bound, regal splendour of Theseus and Hippolyta; the homespun vulgarity of Bottom and the workmen; the ephemeral delicacy of the fairies. The changes in mood as each group takes centre stage, and the contrasts when their worlds meet, gives each scene a subtly different atmosphere.

*Think about how daylight and darkness change our attitudes towards what we see and hear.*

The action of the play is divided by time and location. According to the opening lines, there are four days from the start of the play to the wedding day though in fact there are only three clearly distinguishable days. This need not bother us unduly since the error makes no difference to the action or to our understanding of the events. The opening scene is in daylight, as is the latter part of Act IV Scene 1 when Theseus wakes the four lovers. Theseus embodies the ideas of maturity, stability and reason and these qualities thrive in the light when things are seen clearly. The main body of the action takes place in the darkness of a wood at night. Unlike the wakeful clarity of the daylight scenes, these woodland scenes contain impish mischief, immature behaviour, irrational actions and confusion.

*All drama, even comedy, relies on conflict for real effect.*

Although it is clearly a **comedy** (see Literary Terms), the play contains elements which suggest potential danger or tragedy. At the very start of the play we are reminded of the previous conflict between Theseus and Hippolyta. The argument between Egeus and Hermia immediately shows up the rifts in family life. Helena betrays her close friend and the conflict that is created between the four lovers leads to threats and violent quarrels. Yet we are kept aware that all these potentially harmful situations are being observed, monitored and controlled. Oberon ensures that Puck will keep Lysander and Demetrius apart and that each lover will end up with the right partner. The quarrel between Oberon and Titania is used as a springboard for the tangled chain of events that follows. Yet even that quarrel, which has such terrible consequences for humankind, leads not to bloodshed but to the ridiculously funny situation of Titania falling in love with Bottom and his ass's head. So the play has progressed from the happy thoughts of the royal wedding to a series of conflicts and confusions. All conflicts which have flourished in the night are resolved harmoniously by the time dawn breaks. These conflicts are not out of place in comedy. Drama needs to reflect life, and conflict is an integral part of life. When everything is resolved and we have a happy ending the earlier conflicts make that happiness more complete

The workmen's performance of 'Pyramus and Thisbe' brings an element of **farce** (see Literary Terms) to round off the proceedings. Their play is based on a tragic subject, but their inept performance creates a humorous response which removes any tragic effect. Rather as in *A Midsummer Night's Dream* the potential for tragedy never becomes a reality, and the good humour at the start of the play is restored and increased. To emphasise the happiness of the ending the fairies arrive to bless and protect the newly-weds.

The play's tangled structure creates the atmosphere of a dream, and in a sense that is what all theatre does – presents us with an illusion that we temporarily see as reality.

# CHARACTERS

## THESEUS

*Regal*
*Firm*
*Sensitive*
*Kind*
*Brave*
*Passionate*
*Fair-minded*
*Practical*

Theseus, in Greek legend, was a great hero and a brave warrior who did a great deal to improve the way that Greek society worked, giving each citizen responsibilities and duties as well as rights. In the play, he is presented as a good example of what a sixteenth-century ruler should be. He is strong and heroic; he is aware of his responsibility for maintaining good order and upholding the law; he is thoughtful when making decisions and approaches his duties in a kindly way; he supports the arts and is also a keen sportsman.

In his dealings with Egeus and Hermia we see his firmness in upholding Egeus's rights under the law, but we also see how his suggestion of a lesser penalty than death offers Hermia some hope and calms a dangerous situation. Later in the play, when it is clear that Demetrius no longer wants to marry Hermia, Theseus allows his common sense to dictate his actions. Again, he calms the situation and seems, after the chaos and irrationality of the night, to be the voice of reason that restores order to the events. His decision that the four young lovers may marry the partners of their choice is also an indication of the influence that his love for Hippolyta has had upon him. Despite his rather sceptical dismissal of the overactive imaginations of lovers, whom he groups with poets and madmen, it is clear that Theseus is himself somewhat romantic and passionate. His impatience for his wedding to Hippolyta, the various terms of endearment that he uses towards her – and the list of his former lovers – show that other side to his character. His kindness is revealed early on in the play when he shows sympathy towards Hermia and seems prepared to take Egeus aside for a calm discussion of the situation. Later in the play that same quality is evident in the generous attitude he has towards the well-intentioned efforts of his subjects, especially the workmen's inept production of a play. He joins in the humorous remarks of the courtiers, but his humour is gentle and his thanks to the men at the end of the play is sincere.

In the course of the play, Theseus performs a number of important functions. He is the upholder of the law, a reasoning and flexible spokesman for calm and common sense, a restorer of balance and fairness and a defender of honest effort.

## HIPPOLYTA

*Brave*
*Sensitive*
*Thoughtful*
*Loving*
*Humorous*

Hippolyta was herself a heroic character. She had been the queen of the Amazons and had been defeated in battle by Theseus. In some versions of the story she was ravaged by Theseus and ran away from him, but in other versions they married and lived happily. It is not surprising that Shakespeare chose the happier version! Her qualities of kindness, bravery, regal bearing, good humour and obedience to a higher authority suit her for the role as it would have been seen by an Elizabethan audience.

With Theseus, Hippolyta represents a more mature form of love than the impulsive, youthful romanticism of the four lovers. She is more reconciled to waiting for the wedding day than Theseus is. She has rather more sympathy for the story told by the lovers. Her sensitivity, insight and natural warmth lead her to think that their tale is something more than a figment of the imagination.

Those same qualities affect her reaction to the proposal that the court should see the workmen's play. She is concerned that they will make fools of themselves because she does not really believe that they are capable of anything so ambitious. As she watches their play she is aware that it is 'the silliest stuff' (V.1.208) that she has ever heard, yet her humorous comments are, like those of Theseus, gentle and she is quick to offer Moonshine some praise when his distress at the interruptions becomes clear.

## THE LOVERS

While we need to consider each of the four young lovers as individuals, we can also see that they work dramatically as a group. They represent a more romantic, volatile and passionate side of love to that we see in Theseus and Hippolyta. Some people feel that these four characters lack depth, and that they are, therefore, easily confused with each other. They certainly do share several characteristics. The girls are both romantic, both dote on the man of their choice, both become confused and argumentative. The two young men both become victims of an illusion of love, both turn their backs on the girl they have once loved, both fight for Hermia and then for Helena, both speak in a similarly exaggerated romantic way. For the purposes of this play such similarities are no real problem. Yes, they can lead to confusion, but the group of four lovers is a symbol of young love and their language is that of Elizabethan love poetry. In this way they are quite an effective way for Shakespeare to present his theme of young love, a theme that does not depend upon individuals.

## HERMIA

*Short*

*Dark*

*Passionate*

*Stubborn*

*Quick-tempered*

We learn that Hermia has dark hair, that she is shorter than Helena and that she is regarded as being beautiful. The name Hermia is derived from Hermes, the messenger of the gods, who was also known as Mercury. The name is appropriate as a **characternym** (see Literary Terms) since she changes mood quickly and so she is a 'mercurial' character. She is the first of the four lovers to come to our attention. We see her in dispute with her father who considers her to be disobedient, wilful and stubborn. Many people today can readily sympathise with her disobedience and with her decision to run away from Athens in order to marry Lysander. To the Elizabethans, however, such disobedient and reckless behaviour would have been a cause for disapproval. In the woods she shows modesty in not allowing Lysander to lie down too closely to her. She shows considerable spirit in her verbal attack on Demetrius when she thinks he has killed Lysander, and that spirit is again evident in her fury at what she sees as Helena's underhanded plot to steal Lysander from her. This spirit is an echo of the defiance and self-confidence we have seen in her stand against her father and in her willingness to run away with Lysander. As an audience we see her fury in the woods as amusing, especially when she bases her attack on Helena on a belief that it is the difference in their height that has led Lysander to love Helena.

## HELENA

*Tall*
*Fair*
*Loving*
*Timid*

Helena's name perhaps reminds us of Helen of Troy, the beautiful woman whose abduction started the ten year Trojan War. The name means 'light', and this appropriate since she has a fair complexion and is supposed to be regarded as being as beautiful as Hermia. Unlike Hermia, Helena is rather timid. She lacks Hermia's self-confidence, which is understandable since she has been wooed and then rejected by Demetrius. She dotes on Demetrius so much that she is willing to betray her best friend's secret, to follow Demetrius into the woods and to beg him to treat her like a dog, to beat her rather than to ignore her. Her loyalty to Demetrius never really changes. She suffers confusion and pain when she thinks that the other three are making fun of her and this makes her somewhat more vulnerable and sympathetic than Hermia. It is worth considering how you feel about her happiness at the end of the play. She has got back her lover, Demetrius, but he is still under the influence of Oberon's spell so that, unlike Hermia who has a true love, Helena is left only with a love that is a sort of illusion. Does that make her an object of ridicule or one of sympathy?

## LYSANDER

*Romantic*
*Outspoken*
*Passionate*
*Witty*

The account which Egeus gives of how Lysander had 'stolen' Hermia's affections shows us that he is a romantic person whose approach to Hermia has been sensitive and determined. He is a wealthy young man whose witty comments during the performance of 'Pyramus and Thisbe' show him to be at home in the refined atmosphere of the court. If it were not for Egeus's unexplained dislike of him, he would seem a most eligible suitor. He shows no fear of Egeus, or of

Theseus. He states his case in a forthright and outspoken manner and he is not slow to point out the poor behaviour of Demetrius who has led Helena on and then dropped her for Hermia. Lysander is keen to make it clear that he is faithful in his love – though we know that future events will temporarily change this. His disdain for Demetrius is shown early on when he says that since Demetrius has the love of Egeus, Demetrius should marry him and leave Hermia to Lysander. That disdain continues in their various meetings in the woods. The two men are reconciled at the end of the play, but not before Lysander has accepted the blustering challenge which Demetrius has made.

Lysander's loving nature and his romantic plan to elope tend to put us on his side. When he is under the influence of the love-juice, his hateful contempt for the devoted Hermia seems all the more cruel, but it is a useful reminder of how easily the affections of the young can be swayed.

Demetrius

Demetrius is a rather less likeable character than is Lysander. Though he has the support of Egeus, the revelation that he has previously expressed his love for Helena and has now rejected her makes us feel he is fickle and has behaved badly. Unlike Lysander, Demetrius is not a faithful lover. It is interesting that Theseus should want to talk to him as well as to Egeus at the end of the first scene. The negative view that we have of him is deepened by his treatment of Helena. Far from being grateful to her for the information about Hermia's elopement, he treats Helena badly. He abuses her and threatens her so that we find him callous, selfish and uncaring.

*Self-centred*
*Hot-headed*
*Deceitful*
*Cruel*
*Passionate*

In the first part of the play Demetrius appears somewhat serious and certainly unattractive. His emotions in the woods seem to stem from a sense of being thwarted rather than from a genuine love of Hermia. When he is bewitched and falls in love with Helena the unreal nature of that love is reflected in the exaggerated nature of his language. He does become a figure of fun, and by the end of the play is a much more sympathetic character who, like Lysander, amuses us with his witty comments on the workmen's performance of their play. It is as well to remember that he remains under the influence of the love-juice, so that his love for Helena is not a natural love but one that has been forced upon him. Similarly we could think that his more jovial nature is a side-effect of the spell. Whether we think it fair on Helena and Demetrius that his love is really an illusion, it does seem that they are happy, and we might well consider that Oberon has done them a favour in giving them some sort of happiness. If we do feel that, it is probably more because we want Helena to be happy than out of any desire that Demetrius should feel like that!

# EGEUS

*Old*
*Stern*
*Narrow-minded*
*Determined*

Hermia's father is a rather narrow-minded. He has an authoritarian view of his position as a father, and he expects complete obedience from his daughter. He has little sympathy for young love. His insistence upon demanding the harshest penalty of the law – death for his disobedient daughter – seems cruel and unnatural. He is not a strongly drawn character, but he represents an older generation that contrasts with the exuberant and more wilful younger generation. Dramatically he provides a springboard for the elopement and for all the events in which the four young lovers become involved.

## THE WORKMEN

These may be considered as a group. They are simple men, and their simplicity is reflected by the descriptions of them as 'hempen homespuns' (III.1.70), 'rude mechanicals' (III.2.9), 'hard-handed men' (V.1.72), who are 'clowns' (see the stage directions at the beginning of Act III Scene 1) dismissed by Puck as being of 'that barren sort' (III.2.13). Despite these unflattering descriptions, as a group they represent honest toil, decency, loyalty and endeavour. We are amused by their antics and by their naïvety, but we are intended to share Theseus's view that they are worthy of praise because their intentions are good and their efforts are sincere.

Each of the men is identified by a name and a trade, and each has something that makes him different from the others. Peter Quince is a carpenter and he is also the one who has written the play and who is trying to organise the rehearsals. Quines or quince was the name given to blocks of wood, but a quince is also a fruit, noted for its sharp taste, which was popularly used for making jam. Peter Quince behaves at times in a sharp way and his attempts to put on a play could also be said to land the workmen in a jam. Although he becomes a little irritated by Bottom's attempts to run things, he does generally remain tolerant. His flattering reasons why Bottom must play the part of Pyramus are a good example of his tact. Francis Flute, the bellows-mender, and like a bellows a flute is something that works by a sort of wind power. Wind is insubstantial, and really so is Francis Flute. He is quite a young man. It is natural that he should be chosen to play the part of Thisbe, but as he is proud of the fact that he is now in a position to grow a beard we can understand his reluctance to shave it off and play the part of a woman. Tom Snout is a tinker, that is someone who mends pots and pans; part of a pot would have been the spout or snout. At first he

is asked to take the part of Pyramus's father, but the
workmen's concerns over making the wall seem real
means that he ends up playing Wall. Snug is a joiner,
and he would be expected to make the wooden joints fit
snugly. He describes himself as 'slow of study' (I.2.63)
and Quince may have recognised that fact by casting
Snug as the lion, a part that required no lines to be
learned. Robin Starveling is a tailor. Tailors were
caricatured as being miserly and prepared to rob their
customers by charging them for more cloth than they
had actually used. He is cast as Thisbe's mother, but his
part is changed to that of Moonshine as a result of the
men's concern for making the play seem real. Starveling
is considerably put out by the interruptions that occur
during their performance.

## BOTTOM

*Keen*
*Energetic*
*Simple*
*Honest*
*Open*
*Friendly*

Bottom is a weaver by trade, and there are several
references to that trade in the play. He is far more
developed as a character than the other workmen, and
it would be as well to consider him in greater detail. He
is a boisterous character who is full of enthusiasm and
self-confidence when he is with his fellow workers.
That self-confidence suffers a set-back when they run
away from him, but it returns quickly when Titania
expresses her love and the fairies show him such
attention. It is that same self-confidence which lets him
believe in his ability as an actor and which leads him to
correct Theseus's comment on what might happen next
in the workmen's performance of 'Pyramus and Thisbe'.
As the central character among the workmen he links
their activities with the world of the court and with the
world of the fairies.

Bottom is a thoroughly honest, if sometimes misguided,
character. He is a simple man and that simplicity is
apparent in the contrast between himself and the

majestic Titania. The pleasure he feels at the attention he receives from the fairies is touching, as is the politeness with which he conducts himself. The other workmen regard him highly. They listen to his suggestions, they are impressed by what they see as his considerable acting ability, they refer to him as 'Bully' (III.1.7) which is a term of endearment and they believe he has 'the best wit of any handicraft man in Athens' (IV.2.9–10). Bottom is at the centre of the funniest scenes in the play. When he wakes up after his experiences with Titania he finds it difficult to separate reality from illusion. This is just what he does when they are rehearsing and performing their play. His comment that he will get Quince to write the story and call it 'Bottom's Dream' perhaps reflects Shakespeare's awareness that many people will see Bottom as the central figure of the play. Whether you will be one of those people by the time you have finished considering all aspects of the play remains to be seen.

### OBERON

As the King of the Fairies Oberon represents power in his world in much the same way that Theseus does in the human world. Oberon, however, uses his power rather differently from the way that Theseus uses his. Oberon is more volatile, and his first words, 'Ill met by moonlight, proud Titania' (II.1.60), are a stark contrast to Theseus's words of love. While Theseus is a thoughtful, rational ruler who brings a sense of order and calm, Oberon is a creator of dreams, someone who works in the realms of imagination and whose mischievous use of power brings chaos and confusion.

Oberon is very much a creature of the night. There is a darkness to his character which can make him rather frightening. He is jealous of Titania because she has the

*Imperious*
*Influential*
*Magical*
*Jealous*
*Mischievous*

boy and he wants the boy for his page. His jealousy has caused havoc in nature and his plan to get the boy involves making a fool of Titania. He is a creature of contradictions. We see that he expects to get his own way and that he is prepared to be ruthless in his use of mysterious powers to ensure that he does get his own way. Yet he is capable of feeling sympathy and compassion. He releases Titania from the spell as soon as his objective is accomplished, and it is his sympathy for Helena's treatment by Demetrius that leads him to act on her behalf. He can create a spell which has the potential to harm Titania, yet he can also cast a spell that will protect an unborn child from harm.

Oberon has considerable powers. He can see what others, even Puck, can not and he has observed the gods going about their business. He has a deep knowledge and understanding of the workings of the powers of herbs and plants and of nature. When he describes the change that gave 'love in idleness' (II.1.168) its powers, the mermaid riding on a dolphin's back, the movement of the sea, we recognise that he is so close to nature that he seems a part of it. Oberon displays certain human traits; he is capable of jealousy, anger, pity and mischief. But while he may influence events in the world of men he is not a part of that world. He is a dream figure whose strange combination of goodness and mischief, compassion and vengeance is as magical as his power. The power of that magic is reflected in the power of the language that he uses.

## TITANIA

*Regal*
*Proud*
*Beautiful*
*Caring*
*Passionate*

Titania is the Queen of the Fairies. Oberon describes her as 'proud' (II.1.60) because she has refused to agree to his demand to hand over the Indian boy. Her reasons, however, seem to make some sense, and they suggest that she wants to protect the boy in order to repay the loyalty that the boy's mother had displayed. She is prepared to stand up to Oberon. When he chides her with 'Tarry, rash wanton! Am I not thy lord?' (II.1.63) she responds rather ambiguously with 'Then I must be thy lady' (II.1.64). Oberon's language can be moving and magical, and Titania's language is beautifully poetic. There is an underlying sensuality in the poetry of her language, and she is a passionate creature who expresses her emotions in a physical way. The intimacy with which she treats Bottom highlights the sensual side of her nature, but the scenes with Bottom also highlight the difference between his 'mortal grossness' (III.1.151) and her delicate beauty.

Titania's quarrel with Oberon has caused destruction in nature, and Titania's comments about the natural beauty of the world suggest she is in touch with nature and with its beauty. She sends her fairies to improve the appearance of plants and flowers, and to fight against unpleasant creatures. Under the spell of the love-juice she degrades herself by her devotion to Bottom, but because Bottom is himself such a likeable character there is no real harm done. We are pleased when her senses are restored and when the quarrel between herself and Oberon is resolved. The affection and harmony that these two show at the end of the play once again shows how a love that has come through a time of adversity is perhaps a stronger, richer love.

## PUCK

*Mischievous*
*A joker*
*Loyal to Oberon*
*Sees humans as*
*fools*

Strictly speaking the character is Robin Goodfellow who is a Puck, an impish spirit from English folklore. He has none of the dignity of Titania or Oberon, and from our first meeting with him we realise that he delights in mischief and trickery. Puck steers clear of emotional entanglements, unlike all the other main characters who become deeply involved in each other's

lives. He interferes with the lives of others purely for the mischief that he can cause. He enjoys creating the circumstances in which ridiculous events and behaviour are inevitable. He sometimes acts under the direct instructions of his master, Oberon, but there are suggestions that he has an independent mind. Oberon himself says Puck 'commitest thy knaveries wilfully' (III.2.346) and the trick of putting an ass's head on Bottom was certainly his own idea. Puck loves practical jokes. In Act II Scene 1 we have descriptions of some of his jokes from himself and the fairy that he meets. He is a powerful creature who can 'put a girdle round about the earth / In forty minutes' (II.1.175–6), can change his appearance and voice and can perform dramatic transformations of living creatures. While he claims that 'those things do best please me / That befall preposterously' (III.2.120–1) we might find it hard to really like Puck or to fully share his pleasure in his tricks because, unlike Oberon, he lacks any feelings of compassion. His loyalty to Oberon is, however, beyond question, and when he mistakes Lysander for Demetrius it is an honest mistake. Although Puck is certainly irresponsible, the control that Oberon exercises means that Puck is not only instrumental in causing the chaos and confusion among the four human lovers but also instrumental in protecting them from real harm and finally bringing them to a happy state of harmony.

## THE FAIRIES

Peaseblossom, Cobweb, Moth and Mustardseed are the four fairies mentioned by name. They are loyal followers of Titania who obey her wishes and spend their time helping Nature. Their names are all taken from natural objects. They are attentive to Bottom, though they must see what a ridiculous creature he is.

# LANGUAGE & STYLE

*Shakespeare's use of language gives us real clues about who is speaking and about what is happening.*

The language in Shakespeare's plays is of major importance. Actors in Elizabethan times relied upon the delivery of the words, rather than on the use of gesture or facial expression, to bring out the characters they were playing. The action of the play, as well as its attraction, was to be found in the flow of the language and the sort of language that Shakespeare uses at any one time in his play is a strong indication of the themes as well as of the characters. Shakespeare uses **poetic verse, blank verse** and **prose** (see Literary Terms) for his dialogue. The way in which the language reflects the speakers social standing is apparent when we notice that the courtiers usually speak in blank verse, while the workmen speak in prose. When the workmen perform their play we notice that it is written in verse. This use of verse should indicate the aristocratic nature of the characters of Pyramus and Thisbe but the poor quality of the verse actually emphasises that the workmen are pretending to be what they are not.

The courtiers mainly use unrhymed **iambic pentameter** (see Literary Terms), or blank verse. Each line contains ten syllables divided into five pairs of syllables. The word 'iambic' tells us that these pairs of syllables, or 'feet', each have an unstressed syllable followed by a stressed syllable. You will, however, notice that there are many variations to this and that few of the lines conform completely to this rigid structure. There are many reasons for this. Sometimes Shakespeare might want to emphasise a particular word and the change in stress pattern helps him to do this. At other times you will notice that one character's speech ends on a short line and that the next character's speech begins with another short line. This can indicate, for example, two sides to a quarrel as in Act I Scene 1 where when Hermia responds to Theseus's observation that 'Demetrius is a worthy gentleman' (I.1.52) we have:

HERMIA: So is Lysander.

THESEUS:                    In himself he is;
But in this kind, wanting your father's voice,
The other must be held the worthier. (I.1.53–5)

This same device can indicate two characters working closely together, as in Act II Scene 1 when Puck returns with the flower and says 'Ay, there it is.' And Oberon responds 'I pray thee give it me' (II.1.248).

*Shakespeare's plays show us what a wonderful and versatile poet he was.*

We must also realise that an entire play written in perfectly rhythmical and unrhymed pentameters would be rather tedious! Early on when Hermia and Lysander are alone and discussing their love for each, starting at Act I Scene 1 line 171, Shakespeare introduces **rhyming couplets** (see Literary Terms) that add a more romantic note. The simple couplet form accentuates the innocence as well as the love of these two. When Titania uses rhyming couplets in her expressions of love for Bottom, those rhymes emphasise Titania's delicate and sensuous nature. By contrast the rhymes used by Lysander (Act II Scene 2) and by Demetrius (Act III Scene 2) to express love for Helena are so extravagant that they emphasise the lack of substance that exists in the illusion of love.

Shakespeare's language can, at times, seem to be almost overloaded with literary devices. He uses **puns, antithesis, alliteration** and a variety of **imagery** (see Literary Terms) as well as subtle repetitions, or semi-repetitions of lines to create emphasis. Examples of the pun can be found not only in the somewhat crude link between Bottom's name and the head of an ass, but in Demetrius's assertion that he is 'wood within this wood' (II.1.192). Examples of antithesis are found when Helena says she will 'make a heaven of hell' (II.1.243) and when Theseus reads out the description of the workmen's play (V.1.57–60). Alliteration may be noticed in such lines as Theseus's instruction to Hermia to 'Fit your fancies to your father's will' (I.1.118) and, much more comically, in Quince's **Prologue** (see Literary Terms) when he says: 'Whereat with blade – with bloody, blameful blade – / He bravely broached his boiling bloody breast' (V.1.145–6).

Much of Shakespeare's imagery derives from the references to Greek mythology where, for example, Diana is a symbol of chastity. But he also uses **metaphor** (see Literary Terms) effectively; Lysander refers to Hermia variously as a 'tawny Tartar' (III.2.263), a 'cat' (III.2.260) and a 'serpent' (III.2.261), while Hermia retaliates by accusing Helena of being a 'juggler' (III.2.283), a 'canker-blossom' (III.2.283)and a 'thief of love' (III.2.284).

Though the events of the play sometimes seem dangerous and threatening, and there is considerable dramatic tension at times, the knowledge that there is a power that can resolve things happily in the end enables the comic aspects of the play to dominate. The exaggerated language of the lovers and the workmen's awkward attempts at verse are clear pointers to the comedy which is the essence of the play.

# PART FOUR

# STUDY SKILLS

## HOW TO USE QUOTATIONS

One of the secrets of success in writing essays is the way you use quotations. There are five basic principles:

- Put inverted commas at the beginning and end of the quotation
- Write the quotation exactly as it appears in the original
- Do not use a quotation that repeats what you have just written
- Use the quotation so that it fits into your sentence
- Keep the quotation as short as possible

Quotations should be used to develop the line of thought in your essays.

Your comment should not duplicate what is in your quotation. For example:

> **Lysander tells Helena that Demetrius loves Hermia not Helena, 'Demetrius loves her, and he loves not you'.**

Far more effective is to write:

> **Lysander tells Helena that Demetrius loves Hermia 'and he loves not you'.**

Always lay out the lines as they appear in the text. For example:

> **When Demetrius wakes he falls instantly in love with Helena, declaring:**
> **'O Helen, goddess, nymph, perfect, divine –**
> **To what, my love, shall I compare thine eyne?'**

However, the most sophisticated way of using the writer's words is to embed them into your sentence:

> **Puck describes how he came across a 'crew of patches, rude mechanicals' rehearsing a play near where Titania was sleeping.**

When you use quotations in this way, you are demonstrating the ability to use text as evidence to support your ideas - not simply including words from the original to prove you have read it.

Everyone writes differently. Work through the suggestions given here and adapt the advice to suit your own style and interests. This will improve your essay-writing skills and allow your personal voice to emerge.

The following points indicate in ascending order the skills of essay writing:

- Picking out one or two facts about the story and adding the odd detail
- Writing about the text by retelling the story
- Retelling the story and adding a quotation here and there
- Organising an answer which explains what is happening in the text and giving quotations to support what you write

............................................................

- Writing in such a way as to show that you have thought about the intentions of the writer of the text and that you understand the techniques used
- Writing at some length, giving your viewpoint on the text and commenting by picking out details to support your views
- Looking at the text as a work of art, demonstrating clear critical judgement and explaining to the reader of your essay how the enjoyment of the text is assisted by literary devices, linguistic effects and psychological insights; showing how the text relates to the time when it was written

The dotted line above represents the division between lower and higher level grades. Higher-level performance begins when you start to consider your response as a reader of the text. The highest level is reached when you offer an enthusiastic personal response and show how this piece of literature is a product of its time.

*Coursework essay*

Set aside an hour or so at the start of your work to plan what you have to do.

- List all the points you feel are needed to cover the task. Collect page references of information and quotations that will support what you have to say. A helpful tool is the highlighter pen: this saves painstaking copying and enables you to target precisely what you want to use.
- Focus on what you consider to be the main points of the essay. Try to sum up your argument in a single sentence, which could be the closing sentence of your essay. Depending on the essay title, it could be a statement about a character: Of all the characters in *A Midsummer Night's Dream*, Helena is the one with whom we can most easily sympathise because, being the most steadfast in her love, she suffers the most and yet still ends up with someone who does not really love her of his own free will; an opinion about setting: Shakespeare set much of the play in a moonlit wood to emphasise the mysterious, frightening and dream-like qualities of the events; or a judgement on a theme: I think that the main theme of *A Midsummer Night's Dream* is love because most of the characters in the play experience this emotion in one form or another.
- Make a short essay plan. Use the first paragraph to introduce the argument you wish to make. In the following paragraphs develop this argument with details, examples and other possible points of view. Sum up your argument in the last paragraph. Check you have answered the question.
- Write the essay, remembering all the time the central point you are making.
- On completion, go back over what you have written to eliminate careless errors and improve expression. Read it aloud to yourself, or, if you are feeling more confident, to a relative or friend.

If you can, try to type your essay, using a word processor. This will allow you to correct and improve your writing without spoiling its appearance.

*Examination essay*

The essay written in an examination often carries more marks than the coursework essay even though it is written under considerable time pressure.

In the revision period build up notes on various aspects of the text you are using. Fortunately, in acquiring this set of York Notes on *A Midsummer Night's Dream*, you have made a prudent beginning! York Notes are set out to give you vital information and help you to construct your personal overview of the text.

Make notes with appropriate quotations about the key issues of the set text. Go into the examination knowing your text and having a clear set of opinions about it.

In most English Literature examinations, you can take in copies of your set books. This is an enormous advantage although it may lull you into a false sense of security. Beware! There is simply not enough time in an examination to read the book from scratch.

*In the examination*

- Read the question paper carefully and remind yourself what you have to do.
- Look at the questions on your set texts to select the one that most interests you and mentally work out the points you wish to stress.
- Remind yourself of the time available and how you are going to use it.
- Briefly map out a short plan in note form that will keep your writing on track and illustrate the key argument you want to make.
- Then set about writing it.
- When you have finished, check through to eliminate errors.

*To summarise,*
*these are the*
*keys to success:*

- **Know the text**
- **Have a clear understanding of and opinions on the storyline, characters, setting, themes and writer's concerns**
- **Select the right material**
- **Plan and write a clear response, continually bearing the question in mind**

# SAMPLE ESSAY PLAN

A typical essay question on *A Midsummer Night's Dream* is followed by a sample essay plan in note form. This does not represent the only answer to the question, merely one answer. Do not be afraid to include your own ideas, and leave out some of those in the sample! Remember that quotations are essential to prove and illustrate the points you make.

**To what extent is Theseus presented as a good ruler?**

Such a question anticipates a carefully focused response. To show 'to what extent' you will need to consider:

- What might be regarded as desirable qualities in a ruler
- Whether Theseus demonstrates these qualities
- The historical context of the play
- The role of Theseus within the context of the play
- His behaviour in contrast to the behaviour of others

*Introduction*

This should clearly outline how you are going to deal with the question, and could include a brief idea of how you will interpret the key term 'good ruler'. You could list the qualities which would have been considered desirable in Elizabethan times – and perhaps contrast them with the duties of a modern day ruler.

*First impressions*

How our impressions of Theseus are first created:

- He opens the play, which gives him an immediately dominant position
- His love for Hippolyta gives him humanity

| | |
|---|---|
| *Theseus as upholder of the law* | • His support of Egeus shows support of the law<br>• He sees the law as of first importance<br>• He appears to be harsh |
| *His gentler nature* | • His offer of an alternative penalty to death suggests he is fair-minded<br>• He approaches problems calmly – he is judicious<br>• His language is measured and thoughtful<br>• He offers Hermia time to decide<br>• He takes Egeus and Demetrius aside to talk to them about the situation<br>• Towards the end of the play he overrules Egeus and lets the four lovers marry for love<br>• He is approachable – even Bottom feels he may talk to him directly |
| *Theseus as a well-rounded man* | • He enjoys 'royal' pursuits – we see him hunting<br>• His description of the sound of the hounds suggests an interest in music<br>• He is amused when he discovers the four lovers asleep together<br>• He is a patron of the arts, encouraging his subjects to perform their play<br>• He has a sense of humour, making witty remarks during the play but<br>• He appreciates honest effort and will try not to hurt the feelings of others |
| *Conclusion* | Draw together all the material that you have used in the main body of your essay, but do not simply reiterate everything you have written. Show whether Theseus matched up to the qualities you had listed in your introduction. Try to add something extra to give your reader something to think about, e.g. that Shakespeare helps us to appreciate Theseus's qualities as a good ruler by providing us with Oberon as a contrast. |

This is by no means an exhaustive or definitive answer to the question. However, looked at in conjunction with the general notes on Essay Writing, it does show you the way in which your mind should be working in order to produce a reasonably thorough essay.

# FURTHER QUESTIONS

Make a plan as shown above and attempt these questions.

1 How might a modern production of *A Midsummer Night's Dream* differ from an Elizabethan one?

2 Examine the characters of Hermia and Helena. Show in what ways they differ and in what ways they are similar.

3 What different aspects of love do you see as important in the play?

4 Does Shakespeare's use of unpleasant and possibly threatening scenes add to or spoil our enjoyment of the comedy in this play?

5 In what ways is this play about 'dreams'?

6 How do events support Lysander's claim that 'The course of true love never did run smooth'?

7 Are there any similarities between the fairies and the humans in this play?

8 If you were directing a production of this play how would you bring out the humour in Act V?

9 Oberon describes Puck as a 'mad spirit'. In what ways does his reputation and behaviour support that description?

10 How might the play be said to suggest that Shakespeare only saw love as an illusion?

11 Show how Shakespeare's use of verse and prose helps us to a better understanding of the events and the characters.

12 Bottom is often thought of as the central character of this play. How justified do you consider that view to be?

PART FIVE

# CULTURAL CONNECTIONS

## BROADER PERSPECTIVES

### SHAKESPEARE'S LIFE AND TIMES

To understand Shakespeare in the context of the Elizabethan world it would be useful to find out more about that time. The way people dress can often indicate what they consider important, and you can see examples of Elizabethan 'fashion statements' in portraits of the time. The National Portrait Gallery in London has some excellent paintings which clearly show how the Elizabethans loved to display their wealth and status through their beautiful, bejewelled and richly decorated clothes – and that is just the men! You will also notice how men of learning and wisdom would have themselves painted surrounded by books, maps, globes and scientific instruments.

W.H. Smith also have a video 'Shakespeare – The Life of William Shakespeare' (Castle Communications Ltd, 1995) which comes with a book, entitled 'William Shakespeare: An Outline of his Life', by Robert E. Hunter. The video and book pack looks at the society in which Shakespeare lived. The newly opened Globe Theatre in London, a reconstruction of the original Elizabethan structure, would be well worth a visit.

### ELIZABETHAN ROMANTIC COMEDY

If you have not read any of Shakespeare's plays before, or if you have only read some of his histories or tragedies, you should have a look at some of Shakespeare's comedies such as *Twelfth Night*, *As You Like It*, *Much Ado About Nothing* or *The Taming of the Shrew*. It might be interesting to compare Shakespeare's handling of the theme of love in *A Midsummer Night's Dream* with the tragic love story of *Romeo and Juliet*. A useful, clearly written book on the subject is *Introducing Shakespeare* by G.B. Harrison (Penguin, 1966).

John Dover Wilson compiled an anthology of writings from the Elizabethan era, *Life in Shakespeare's England* (Macmillan, 1913). The collection gives insights into many relevant topics, though the book is now probably only available in libraries.

A lighter view of the period may be found in the irreverent historical account *The Terrible Tudors* by Terry Deary and Neil Tongue (Scholastic Publications, 1993).

## Video

There is a BBC Video of *A Midsummer Night's Dream* starring Helen Mirren, Peter McEnery and Nigel Davenport. This 1988 production was produced by Jonathan Miller and directed by Elijah Moshinsky.

An animated version was produced for the BBC series 'Shakespeare – The Animated Tales'. This animated version was directed by Robert Saakiants.

There are frequently productions of the play in local theatres and if you have a good repertory company near you then a production would be well worth a visit. Remember that you are studying a play, and plays are meant to be performed and seen – not just read.

**alliteration** a sequence of repeated consonant sounds

**antithesis** opposing or contrasting ideas

**blank verse** unrhymed iambic pentameter the most common Shakespearean poetic form

**characternym** a name that represents its bearer in some appropriate way

**comedy** a broad description for a drama which is intended primarily to entertain the audience and which ends happily for the characters

**farce** a form of humorous drama which uses exaggerated characters, absurd and ridiculous situations and knockabout action to get laughs

**genre** the term for a kind or type of literature, e.g. romantic novel, short story, play

**iamb** the commonest metrical foot in English verse, a weak stress followed by a strong stress, ti-tum

**iambic pentameter** a line of five iambic feet. The most common metrical pattern found in English verse

**imagery** word pictures which help our understanding and interpretation

**irony** saying one thing while meaning another. In dramatic irony the characters are blind to fateful circumstances of which the audience is fully aware, so that what the characters say has an extra meaning for the audience

**lyrical** using the language of lyric poetry, a form that expresses a speaker's thoughts and feelings in a personal and colourful way

**metaphor** a metaphor is the fusing of two different things or ideas; one thing is described as being another thing e.g. 'O, how ripe in show / Thy lips – those Kissing cherries – tempting grow!' III.2.139–40)

**metre** this is the pattern of stressed and unstressed syllables in a line of verse

**oxymoron** a figure of speech in which words of opposite meaning are put together

**poetic verse** a style of speech in Shakespeare's plays using rhyming couplets and having a strong rhythm

**prologue** an introduction to a literary work, or, in the case of a play the speaker of such an introduction

**prose** all writing that is not in verse

**pun** a play on words

**rhyming couplet** a pair of lines that rhyme

**simile** a figure of speech in which one thing is said to be like another, always containing the word 'like' or 'as'

**soliloquy** a speech in which a character in a play speaks directly to the audience – as if thinking aloud about motives, feelings and decisions

**sub-plot** a subsidiary action running parallel with the main plot of a play or novel

# TEST ANSWERS

**TEST YOURSELF (Act I)**

A 1 Egeus *(Scene 1)*
••• 2 Hermia *(Scene 1*
3 Helena *(Scene 1)*
4 Helena *(Scene 1)*
5 Flute *(Scene 2)*
6 Philostrate *(Scene 1)*
7 Hermia *(Scene 1)*
8 Theseus *(Scene 1)*
9 Flute *(Scene 2)*
10 Snug *(Scene 2)*

**TEST YOURSELF (Act II)**

A 1 Titania *(Scene 1)*
••• 2 Oberon *(Scene 1)*
3 Puck *(Scene 1)*
4 Helena *(Scene 2)*
5 Hermia *(Scene 2)*
6 Titania *(Scene 1)*
7 Puck *(Scene 1)*
8 Demetrius *(Scene 1)*
9 Helena *(Scene 1)*
10 Helena *(Scene 2)*

**TEST YOURSELF (Act III)**

A 1 Bottom *(Scene 1)*
••• 2 Puck *(Scene 1)*
3 Quince *(Scene 1)*
4 Puck *(Scene 2)*
5 Helena *(Scene 2)*
6 Bottom *(Scene 1)*

7 Hermia *(Scene 2)*
8 Puck *(Scene 2)*
9 Demetrius *(Scene 2)*
10 Helena *(Scene 2)*

**TEST YOURSELF (Act IV)**

A 1 Bottom *(Scene 1)*
••• 2 Oberon *(Scene 1)*
3 Egeus *(Scene 1)*
4 Demetrius *(Scene 1)*
5 Flute *(Scene 2)*
6 Bottom *(Scene 1)*
7 Titania *(Scene 1)*
8 Bottom *(Scene 1)*
9 Oberon *(Scene 1)*
10 Hermia, Lysander, Helena and
Demetrius *(Scene 1)*

**TEST YOURSELF (Act V)**

A 1 Theseus
••• 2 Philostrate
3 Hippolyta
4 Theseus
5 Bottom as Pyramus
6 Oberon
7 Hermia, Lysander, Helena and
Demetrius
8 Philostrate
9 Hippolyta
10 Bottom as Pyramus
11 Quince as the Prologue

# OTHER TITLES

## GCSE and equivalent levels (£3.50 each)

Maya Angelou
*I Know Why the Caged Bird Sings*

Jane Austen
*Pride and Prejudice*

Alan Ayckbourn
*Absent Friends*

Elizabeth Barrett Browning
*Selected Poems*

Robert Bolt
*A Man for All Seasons*

Harold Brighouse
*Hobson's Choice*

Charlotte Brontë
*Jane Eyre*

Emily Brontë
*Wuthering Heights*

Shelagh Delaney
*A Taste of Honey*

Charles Dickens
*David Copperfield*

Charles Dickens
*Great Expectations*

Charles Dickens
*Hard Times*

Charles Dickens
*Oliver Twist*

Roddy Doyle
*Paddy Clarke Ha Ha Ha*

George Eliot
*Silas Marner*

George Eliot
*The Mill on the Floss*

William Golding
*Lord of the Flies*

Oliver Goldsmith
*She Stoops To Conquer*

Willis Hall
*The Long and the Short and the Tall*

Thomas Hardy
*Far from the Madding Crowd*

Thomas Hardy
*The Mayor of Casterbridge*

Thomas Hardy
*Tess of the d'Urbervilles*

Thomas Hardy
*The Withered Arm and other Wessex Tales*

L.P. Hartley
*The Go-Between*

Seamus Heaney
*Selected Poems*

Susan Hill
*I'm the King of the Castle*

Barry Hines
*A Kestrel for a Knave*

Louise Lawrence
*Children of the Dust*

Harper Lee
*To Kill a Mockingbird*

Laurie Lee
*Cider with Rosie*

Arthur Miller
*The Crucible*

Arthur Miller
*A View from the Bridge*

Robert O'Brien
*Z for Zachariah*

Frank O'Connor
*My Oedipus Complex and other stories*

George Orwell
*Animal Farm*

J.B. Priestley
*An Inspector Calls*

Willy Russell
*Educating Rita*

Willy Russell
*Our Day Out*

J.D. Salinger
*The Catcher in the Rye*

William Shakespeare
*Henry IV Part 1*

William Shakespeare
*Henry V*

William Shakespeare
*Julius Caesar*

William Shakespeare
*Macbeth*

William Shakespeare
*The Merchant of Venice*

William Shakespeare
*A Midsummer Night's Dream*

William Shakespeare
*Much Ado About Nothing*

William Shakespeare
*Romeo and Juliet*

William Shakespeare
*The Tempest*

William Shakespeare
*Twelfth Night*

George Bernard Shaw
*Pygmalion*

Mary Shelley
*Frankenstein*

R.C. Sherriff
*Journey's End*

Rukshana Smith
*Salt on the snow*

John Steinbeck
*Of Mice and Men*

Robert Louis Stevenson
*Dr Jekyll and Mr Hyde*

Jonathan Swift
*Gulliver's Travels*

Robert Swindells
*Daz 4 Zoe*

Mildred D. Taylor
*Roll of Thunder, Hear My Cry*

Mark Twain
*Huckleberry Finn*

James Watson
*Talking in Whispers*

William Wordsworth
*Selected Poems*

*A Choice of Poets*

*Mystery Stories of the Nineteenth Century including The Signalman*

*Nineteenth Century Short Stories*

*Poetry of the First World War*

*Six Women Poets*

## York Notes Advanced (£3.99 each)

Margaret Atwood
*The Handmaid's Tale*

Jane Austen
*Mansfield Park*

Jane Austen
*Persuasion*

Jane Austen
*Pride and Prejudice*

Alan Bennett
*Talking Heads*

William Blake
*Songs of Innocence and of Experience*

Charlotte Brontë
*Jane Eyre*

Emily Brontë
*Wuthering Heights*

Geoffrey Chaucer
*The Franklin's Tale*

Geoffrey Chaucer
*General Prologue to the Canterbury Tales*

Geoffrey Chaucer
*The Wife of Bath's Prologue and Tale*

Joseph Conrad
*Heart of Darkness*

Charles Dickens
*Great Expectations*

John Donne
*Selected Poems*

George Eliot
*The Mill on the Floss*

F. Scott Fitzgerald
*The Great Gatsby*

E.M. Forster
*A Passage to India*

Brian Friel
*Translations*

Thomas Hardy
*The Mayor of Casterbridge*

Thomas Hardy
*Tess of the d'Urbervilles*

Seamus Heaney
*Selected Poems from Opened Ground*

Nathaniel Hawthorne
*The Scarlet Letter*

James Joyce
*Dubliners*

John Keats
*Selected Poems*

Christopher Marlowe
*Doctor Faustus*

Arthur Miller
*Death of a Salesman*

Toni Morrison
*Beloved*

William Shakespeare
*Antony and Cleopatra*

William Shakespeare
*As You Like It*

William Shakespeare
*Hamlet*

William Shakespeare
*King Lear*

William Shakespeare
*Measure for Measure*

William Shakespeare
*The Merchant of Venice*

William Shakespeare
*Much Ado About Nothing*

William Shakespeare
*Othello*

William Shakespeare
*Romeo and Juliet*

William Shakespeare
*The Tempest*

William Shakespeare
*The Winter's Tale*

Mary Shelley
*Frankenstein*

Alice Walker
*The Color Purple*

Oscar Wilde
*The Importance of Being Earnest*

Tennessee Williams
*A Streetcar Named Desire*

John Webster
*The Duchess of Malfi*

W.B. Yeats
*Selected Poems*

Chinua Achebe
*Things Fall Apart*

Edward Albee
*Who's Afraid of Virginia Woolf?*

Margaret Atwood
*Cat's Eye*

Jane Austen
*Emma*

Jane Austen
*Northanger Abbey*

Jane Austen
*Sense and Sensibility*

Samuel Beckett
*Waiting for Godot*

Robert Browning
*Selected Poems*

Robert Burns
*Selected Poems*

Angela Carter
*Nights at the Circus*

Geoffrey Chaucer
*The Merchant's Tale*

Geoffrey Chaucer
*The Miller's Tale*

Geoffrey Chaucer
*The Nun's Priest's Tale*

Samuel Taylor Coleridge
*Selected Poems*

Daniel Defoe
*Moll Flanders*

Daniel Defoe
*Robinson Crusoe*

Charles Dickens
*Bleak House*

Charles Dickens
*Hard Times*

Emily Dickinson
*Selected Poems*

Carol Ann Duffy
*Selected Poems*

George Eliot
*Middlemarch*

T.S. Eliot
*The Waste Land*

T.S. Eliot
*Selected Poems*

Henry Fielding
*Joseph Andrews*

E.M. Forster
*Howards End*

John Fowles
*The French Lieutenant's Woman*

Robert Frost
*Selected Poems*

Elizabeth Gaskell
*North and South*

Stella Gibbons
*Cold Comfort Farm*

Graham Greene
*Brighton Rock*

Thomas Hardy
*Jude the Obscure*

Thomas Hardy
*Selected Poems*

Joseph Heller
*Catch-22*

Homer
*The Iliad*

Homer
*The Odyssey*

Gerard Manley Hopkins
*Selected Poems*

Aldous Huxley
*Brave New World*

Kazuo Ishiguro
*The Remains of the Day*

Ben Jonson
*The Alchemist*

Ben Jonson
*Volpone*

James Joyce
*A Portrait of the Artist as a Young Man*

Philip Larkin
*Selected Poems*

D.H. Lawrence
*The Rainbow*

D.H. Lawrence
*Selected Stories*

D.H. Lawrence
*Sons and Lovers*

D.H. Lawrence
*Women in Love*

John Milton
*Paradise Lost Bks I & II*

John Milton
*Paradise Lost Bks IV & IX*

Thomas More
*Utopia*

Sean O'Casey
*Juno and the Paycock*

George Orwell
*Nineteen Eighty-four*

John Osborne
*Look Back in Anger*

Wilfred Owen
*Selected Poems*

Sylvia Plath
*Selected Poems*

Alexander Pope
*Rape of the Lock and other poems*

Ruth Prawer Jhabvala
*Heat and Dust*

Jean Rhys
*Wide Sargasso Sea*

William Shakespeare
*As You Like It*

William Shakespeare
*Coriolanus*

William Shakespeare
*Henry IV Pt 1*

William Shakespeare
*Henry V*

William Shakespeare
*Julius Caesar*

William Shakespeare
*Macbeth*

William Shakespeare
*Measure for Measure*

William Shakespeare
*A Midsummer Night's Dream*

William Shakespeare
*Richard II*

William Shakespeare
*Richard III*

William Shakespeare
*Sonnets*

William Shakespeare
*The Taming of the Shrew*

William Shakespeare
*Twelfth Night*

William Shakespeare
*The Winter's Tale*

George Bernard Shaw
*Arms and the Man*

George Bernard Shaw
*Saint Joan*

Muriel Spark
*The Prime of Miss Jean Brodie*

John Steinbeck
*The Grapes of Wrath*

John Steinbeck
*The Pearl*

Tom Stoppard
*Arcadia*

Tom Stoppard
*Rosencrantz and Guildenstern are Dead*

Jonathan Swift
*Gulliver's Travels and The Modest Proposal*

Alfred, Lord Tennyson
*Selected Poems*

W.M. Thackeray
*Vanity Fair*

Virgil
*The Aeneid*

Edith Wharton
*The Age of Innocence*

Tennessee Williams
*Cat on a Hot Tin Roof*

Tennessee Williams
*The Glass Menagerie*

Virginia Woolf
*Mrs Dalloway*

Virginia Woolf
*To the Lighthouse*

William Wordsworth
*Selected Poems*

*Metaphysical Poets*